REFUGE

Stories of Restored Lives
in Ridgefield, La Center
and Woodland, WA

Table of Contents

ACKNOWLEDGEMENTS

I would like to thank Brian Thomas for his vision and hard work in making this book a reality. To the brave storytellers, thank you for your boldness and vulnerability in sharing your personal stories.

This book would not have been published without the amazing efforts of our project manager and editor, Samantha Jaquez. Her untiring resolve pushed this project forward and turned it into a stunning victory. Thank you for your great fortitude and diligence. Deep thanks to our incredible editor in chief, Michelle Cuthrell, and executive editor, Jen Genovesi, for all the amazing work they do. I would also like to thank our invaluable proofreader, Melody Davis, for the focus and energy she has put into perfecting our words.

Lastly, I want to extend our gratitude to the creative and very talented Ariana Randle, who designed the beautiful cover for *Refuge: Stories of Restored Lives in Ridgefield, La Center and Woodland, WA.*

Daren Lindley
President and CEO
Good Catch Publishing

The book you are about to read
is a compilation of authentic life stories.
The facts are true, and the events are real.
These storytellers have dealt with crisis, tragedy, abuse
and neglect and have shared their most private moments,
mess-ups and hang-ups in order for others to learn and
grow from them. In order to protect the identities of those
involved in their pasts, the names and details of some
storytellers have been withheld or changed.

INTRODUCTION

Interesting things, scars. Some fade over time. Others become more pronounced. Some appear in places we wish we could hide so no one would see them. Others hide in places no one could find, no one could see, no one could touch — no matter how much we wish somebody would. Some scars exist deep in our hearts and minds, either because of things we have done or things done to us. Our scars reveal our history, our stories. They contribute part of what makes us who we are. If you really want to know someone, ask about his or her scars.

The seven stories in this book come from real people from our very own community. People wounded by loss and fear, neglect and negligence, physical abuse, sexual abuse, mental abuse, drugs and alcohol, pride and prejudice, insecurity, insincerity, hypocrisy, infidelity and divorce. They bear the scars to prove it. As they share their stories, you'll see that their scars are a reminder not just of how they were wounded, but of the fact that they have been healed. Each of these people found refuge right here in our community and in time found healing for their wounds. They share their stories, show their scars, because they want others to know that no matter the wounds, the hurt, the loss, the addiction, the depression, the grief — there is *REFUGE*.

A NEW SONG
The Story of David

Written by Arlene Showalter

"Boss wants to see you in his office." I had just backed my delivery truck up to the loading dock and hopped down to the ground.

"Sure. Thanks." I took the steps two at a time, tapped on the boss' door and entered.

"You wanted to see me?"

"Yes. Do you have anything unusual to report about your run last Wednesday?"

"No. Why?"

"Sure about that? Nothing unusual about the delivery at Bonnie's Restaurant?"

Whatever is he getting at? "Positive. Run went like every other day."

"Every other day, huh?" He snorted. "I'll bet." He looked me straight in the eye.

"David, you're fired."

"*Fired*? Why?"

"I'm pretty sure you know why. Now remove your sorry self from my office."

❧❧❧

REFUGE

Two great people brought me into the world. Maybe three, if you count the doctor. My parents loved their sons and supported us in our learning and growing. Both strove to teach us responsibility, knowing they were raising boys to become men.

"You going to try out for Little League?" Dad asked when I was 7. Dad loved baseball, and we knew who'd control the TV when the Mariners played.

"I'd like to."

"Good. Your mom and I will be there for all your games. You can count on us." They came, both to cheer me on when I made a good play and to cheer me up when I flubbed. I loved the game.

"That's my boy!" Dad jumped up and down in the bleachers as I caught another base hit and tagged the runner out.

Life in a small town in the Pacific Northwest promised to be as fresh and pristine as the air circulating Mount Hood.

Mom and Dad worked hard all week and then partied down with booze to relax on weekends. After a couple of cold ones, Dad relaxed into happy banter, and Mom got testy.

"Hey, hon, you sure look good today."

"What's that supposed to mean?" Mom snapped. "You saying I look ugly the rest of the time?"

"Huh?" Dad blinked a few times. "I'm just trying to pay my wife a compliment."

A NEW SONG

"You're drunk. I'd like to know what you really think when you're *sober.*"

"Drunk?" A scowl chased the smile from Dad's face. "You're drunk. And mean. And not so pretty *now.*"

Time to make myself scarce, I thought as I double-timed it to my bedroom and closed the door. *I hate it when they drink like this. They really are cool parents, until the liquor takes over.*

My folks kept the drinking in the family. Relatives came to our house, or we went to theirs, every weekend.

"We're leaving for Uncle Joe's house in 10 minutes," Mom announced when I was 8.

"Okay, Mom." *Boring. They'll all get smashed, and there won't be a thing to do.*

After hanging around and watching TV, nature bade me to take care of business in Uncle's lavatory.

I parked myself, thinking, *I hope we don't stay too late.* Suddenly, I noticed a magazine sitting next to the toilet. *May as well read.* I yawned. *Can't be any more boring than that stupid TV show.*

I flipped it open, and boredom vanished like mist on the Columbia as gorgeous women peered up at me in strange and tantalizing postures.

Wow, I've never seen anything like this before. So, this is what women look like with no clothes on. I pawed through the *Playboy,* amazed, shocked, pleased and scared at the images smiling back at me.

Months passed, but the memory remained sharp.

"Get ready to go," Mom said while I scarfed down my

Wheaties. "We're leaving for Uncle Joe's in an hour."

Uncle Joe's! I kept my face blasé and spooned another bite of cereal in my mouth, but my mind and heart raced. *Woohoo!*

As soon as the adults had imbibed enough not to notice or care about my absence, I slipped away to the bathroom. *Cool! New magazines.* I flipped through the latest issues, committing to memory every image. *Better not stay too long. I'm toast if somebody catches me.*

"We're going to Uncle Chase's today."

"Do we have to?" *Double boring. Just girls there.*

"They're family." Mom frowned. "It's not the end of the world just because you have to play with *girl* cousins. Girls don't have to be boring, you know. I'm sure they have some nice board games you can play together."

Yeah, right. At 9, my brain refused to fathom such a possibility that girls could be *fun.* I turned up my nose, but kept my mouth shut.

"Come on, let's play," said Lila, also 9. "In my bedroom."

Her sisters followed, twittering and chattering. I dragged my feet like a man to the gallows.

As soon as Lila shut the door, she turned to me. "We want to play doctor."

"*Doctor*? Why?"

She snickered. "We know you're different because we see Mom changing our brother's diaper. We want to check it out. You can play doctor on us, too."

A NEW SONG

My ears pricked up. Real bodies, even girlish bodies, seemed more interesting than the flat magazine photos *Playboy* offered.

"But what about our parents?"

"You don't tell, we won't, either." They all faced me. "Deal?"

"Deal."

After that, I preferred Uncle Chase's to Uncle Joe's, and over the next 10 years, I got to watch my cousins grow toward womanhood "au natural."

෴

"We're going to drive out to Wyoming and visit the Jacksons," Dad announced when I was 12. They'd lived across the street from us before their move east.

"Let's go for a ride in my car," their 18-year-old son, Justin, suggested after we arrived. "I'll show you around town." Later on, as he stopped at a red light, Justin pulled something from under his car seat.

"Take a look at that," he said, tossing me the magazine.

I opened it. The images made *Playboy* look like a first-grader's reading book. My eyes got bigger and bigger.

"Cool, huh?" Justin punched my arm.

෴

"Check it out." Frank held out his lit cigarette. "Go ahead, try it."

REFUGE

Small towns have small schools. Small schools grow big peer pressure because everybody knows everybody. Especially in junior high with fellow 12-year-old kids fumbling our way toward adulthood.

I took a long pull. My throat burned, and I gagged.

"You'll get used to it, David." Frank punched my arm and laughed.

As my lungs adjusted to the abuse, my cravings grew, and by 13, I needed my nicotine fix. Lila and her sisters joined the hunt as we scavenged our parents' ashtrays for discards. A long butt was a great find.

But Grandma, bless her heart, smoked like a fiend and kept cigarette packs scattered all over her home. She looked the other way, while we helped ourselves to her cache.

"Have a drag off this." Lester handed me a toke, where we huddled under a cattle crossing and drank beer. "It'll make you feel super."

Whew, this thing stinks. I tried not to wince. *Can't wimp out in front of my buddies.* I inhaled. *Yuck. Tastes awful, too.* I gasped for breath, and my eyes watered. Then the buzz kicked in. "Whoa. This stuff is great!"

My friends laughed and slapped me on the back. "You'll love it once you get used to it."

Hardworking Dad instilled the same principle in me. I landed my first job, washing dishes in a nursing home, when I hit 16. I set my sights on a cool used white 1962

Dodge Dart. It came with red interior and push-button gears. I dolled it up with baby moon tires.

Yeah, baby, I have arrived.

❧❧❧

"You know my daughter Kellie?" Mrs. Ross worked at the same nursing home.

"Not sure I do. What grade is she in?"

"Ninth, this year."

"Sorry, can't say I do." As a mature junior, I wasn't in the habit of scouting out the underclassmen.

"She knows who you are."

"Oh? That's nice."

"I ride the bus with a really nice girl," Lester told me. "Her name's Kellie Ross."

"Kellie Ross? I work in the same place as her mom."

"You should get to know her. You'd like her."

"Tell you what I'm going to do. I'm going to walk right up to her and kiss her."

"You're nuts."

"Maybe, but that's the plan."

A few days later, as Lester and I headed for the gym, we saw Kellie leave it and come toward us.

"Here's your chance," he whispered, elbowing me in the ribs.

I looked at her with new eyes. *She's cute,* I thought as I executed my plan and kissed her on the mouth. I pulled back. "I'm David."

"I know. I'm Kellie."

She is and always will be the only girl for me.

"See you around."

"Okay." She smiled. *Wow. Love her dimples!*

"Can you get me her phone number?" I asked Lester later that day.

"Sure will."

"Hi, this is David," I said, calling Kellie's house. "Can I talk to Kellie?"

"Kellie," Mr. Ross yelled. "Some guy named *Dufus* wants to talk to you."

We restricted most of our dates to school events — dances and varsity games. Mrs. Ross liked me right away, but Kellie's dad held all potential serious-dates-sniffing-around-his-daughter at bay. His scrutinizing and disapproving eyes seemed to bore straight through my skinny body every time I showed up at his home.

"I have to do something," I told Kellie as my high school graduation approached. "My parents don't care about college, so I know they're not going to pay for it. I think I'd like to try the Navy."

"Whatever you want to do is fine by me."

"This is for you," I said, handing her a little box. In it lay a dainty ring, with a braided band and a tiny diamond nestled in the center of a bow. "I promise you that I'll marry you when I'm done with the Navy."

A NEW SONG

❧❧❧

I enjoyed my last two months of boyhood before handing myself over to the U.S. Navy to make a man of me.

"I'll see you at Christmas," I promised Kellie with a kiss as I left for boot camp in Southern California.

"At Christmas," she agreed.

I survived boot camp, flew home for Christmas and then back to California for further training.

"David, I have bad news." Kellie's voice trembled over the phone when she called me two months after my return.

"What?" I tried to keep my own voice steady as panic gripped my stomach.

"I'm pregnant."

"Are you sure?"

"Yes. I asked my sister to take me to a clinic over in Oregon. The test confirmed that I'm pregnant."

"Good!" I said. "I'll come home and marry you."

"But I'm scared. My dad's going to flip out."

"Don't tell anybody anything. I'll check with my superiors and see if I can get emergency leave."

Kellie met me at the airport a few days later and drove me home.

"We have something to tell you," I said to Mom as we walked in the door.

She looked at Kellie and then me. "I'm going to be a grandma!" she squealed.

"Congratulations, son." Dad stood up and slapped my back.

"I'm so excited." Mom hugged me and then Kellie.

"Can I use your phone?" Kellie asked. "I'm going to have to break the news to my own parents."

"Of course." Mom beamed. "Surely they will be excited, too."

"Mom, maybe." She picked up the phone. "Dad will hit the roof."

"Hello, Mom? This is Kellie." She moved the phone from one hand to the other. "I … uh … I have to tell you something. I'm … pregnant." She dabbed at tears forming in the corner of her eyes. "Yes, I'm sure." Another pause. "You'd do that? Thanks, Mom."

"What did she say?" I asked.

"She said she'd tell my dad when he gets home from work. I'm so scared, David. It's going to be ugly."

Someone knocked on the door a few hours later.

"It's your dad," Mom whispered to Kellie. Then she opened the door. Mr. Ross stepped in. The fire in his eyes dared any of us to intervene.

"Come on," he said, motioning for Kellie to come.

She turned and mouthed, "I'm afraid."

A NEW SONG

The phone rang 30 minutes later. "He's coming to kill you!" My heart pounded at the panic in Kellie's voice. "David, I've never heard him swear in my whole life. He's really, really upset. He dropped me off and said he was going to kill you."

"Oh, okay." *What can I say?* Words refused to form.

The phone rang again 10 minutes later. "He must have changed his mind about killing you," Kellie said. "He's pulling into our driveway right now. I have to go. Bye."

The next morning, Kellie called again. "My dad says he wants to talk to you. He wants you to come here right now."

The moment I pulled into the driveway, Mr. Ross flew out the door, slamming the screen door shut behind him, and started loping toward the large field behind his house. He motioned for me to follow.

Oh, man, this is it. He's going to beat the crap out of me. But I gotta man up and take responsibility for my actions, so here goes. I climbed out of the car and followed him until he stopped in the middle of the field. *Only one of us is going to return from this altercation, and I know it won't be me.*

Mr. Ross whirled to face me. I braced myself for the first punch.

"You love my daughter?" he demanded.

"I do, and I want to take care of her."

He studied me and then swung out one hand. I ducked the blow.

"No, no." He laughed. "I want to *shake* your hand. Believe it or not, I've always liked you, and I think you'd be good for my daughter." He draped an arm around my shoulders, and we walked back to the house together.

"I will tell you this, though. You'll have to wait until Kellie's of age to marry. The State of Washington doesn't allow for her to marry as a minor. And she wants to finish high school."

"That's reasonable."

෨෨෨

I flew back for the wedding one month later. We chose the little church up the street from her house. After a small "dry" reception at her parents' home, we drove over to my parents' place where my family waited to party down.

"Come on, David. We need to get some good stuff." Uncle Chase and Uncle Leon corralled me toward Uncle Leon's car.

"Time to get this party started!" Uncle Chase said, breaking open one of the bottles of Jack Daniels. He tipped the bottle back and then handed it off to me.

"I don't want to drink now," I said.

Uncle Leon mashed the brakes. "Drink up or get out, man," he said.

"Seven miles?"

"Your choice." Uncle Chase handed the bottle over again. He slapped my sailor's hat on my head. "We'll tie your hands behind your back, too."

A NEW SONG

I drank up and was completely wasted by the time we got home. My family howled with glee.

Kellie took me over to the honeymoon suite where she had to sign us in.

Shortly after I got to the room, I flopped on the bed like a ragdoll and passed out.

Kellie and I flew back to California the next day — she, for a one-week honeymoon, and I, to get back to work.

"Here's my place," I said, throwing open the door to the tiny apartment near the ocean. "Welcome home."

My drinking buddies flocked over like the swallows of San Juan Capistrano, and life returned to normal as we passed around one glass pipe filled with hash and inhaled our troubles away.

"I can't believe I married into this," my bride of three days cried.

"What? You're kidding me. We're just relaxing. Lighten up."

"I wasn't raised around booze." She lifted an empty can with two fingers, curled her lip and flipped the can into the garbage. "Or that." She pointed to the bong. "How can you not see how wrong and *illegal* it is?"

I shrugged. *She's pregnant. Her hormones are all out of whack. She'll get over it.*

Kellie returned north to finish school. I frequented bars and strip joints in my free time. My buddies and I drank and got high in my apartment.

"The baby's coming." Kellie called me from the hospital. "How soon can you get here?"

"As soon as the papers clear."

I made it the day after our son, Matt, was born. She graduated high school six weeks later. Then she and Matt joined me in California.

My buddies and I celebrated their arrival with booze and topped it with hash and other hard drugs.

"What's wrong with you?" I yelled at Kellie after she'd retreated to our bedroom and slammed the door shut.

"Do those guys have to come over *every* night?" she demanded. "What about me? What about our son?"

"Nobody's making you stay holed up in here."

"I don't like it. All this drinking and drugs is — wrong."

"Who made you the judge around here?"

She slapped me. I smacked her back.

"This isn't what I signed up for," she said, sobbing.

☙☙☙

My naval career finally ended, and I dry docked for good. I left the military without a backward glance, packed up my little family and returned to the Pacific Northwest.

"We have a job opening where I work," Uncle Darrell told me. "I can put in a good word for you if you want it."

"Sure. Thanks."

I got hired on, and every night after work, Uncle Darrell and I went to the bars to relax. Afterward, I'd stumble home, drunk. I worked, drank and slept — in that order.

"I'm leaving," Kellie said after putting up with my nonsense for a few months. "I'd rather live with my strict father than a stinking drunk."

"What's wrong with the way I live?"

"You don't know?"

"No. I work hard. I don't run around on you. I'm entitled to some relaxation, aren't I?"

She picked up our baby and left.

I called her 40 minutes later.

"You can't leave me like this."

"Why not?"

"We're family — you, me, Matt."

"I'll come back on one condition — you have to promise you'll change."

"I promise."

"And go to church."

"I don't want to dress up like some white-shirt-black-suit-white-socks idiot."

"You don't have to. Lots of churches allow casual dress," she said. "Besides, my dad has a friend who's willing to come over and share the Bible with you."

"I don't want …"

"Then I'm staying right here."

"I'll do it. I promise. Just, come home. Please."

"Hi, I'm William." The man held out his big hand and grinned. "I've freed up my Saturday nights to come and share Jesus with you."

"Come on in." I took his hand. *Still not sure about all*

this, but I don't want to lose Kellie. "We'll sit at the kitchen table. Kellie made a pot of coffee."

"Thank you." He smiled at Kellie and sat down. He placed his Bible on the table and said, "How about if we start with the book of John?"

I shrugged. *Genesis. John. Josiah. They're all the same to me.* "Whatever you suggest is fine by me."

He opened his big dog-eared Bible. "In the beginning was the Word, and the Word was with God and the Word was God."

That sure sounds strange.

"John is talking about Jesus here."

Huh?

"God is a trinity of three equal personages: Father, Jesus and the Holy Spirit. That means Jesus took part in creation. That's what verse 3 says. 'Through him all things were made.'"

"Okay, that makes sense."

"Moving on to verse 4, we see that God sent Jesus as a light to the world. He came to show us God, as a real flesh-and-blood man."

I can handle this, I decided. *It's not too far-fetched.*

William returned the following Saturday.

"We'll read John, chapter 3, today," he said. "This old guy, Nicodemus, wanted to understand how he could approach God, so he went to ask Jesus some questions."

We read about Jesus explaining this crazy concept of being "born again." Even Nicodemus had a problem with that. Jesus kept right on talking to him and revealed why God sent him (Jesus) to the earth in the first place.

"Please read verses 16 and 17," William said.

"Sure. 'For God so loved the world that he gave his one and only son, that whoever believes in him shall not perish but have eternal life. For God did not send his son into the world to condemn the world, but to save the world through him.'"

"You see, David, God sent Jesus to save you."

"Me? What do I need saved from?"

"Aren't you a sinner?"

"Uh, no, I don't think so. I don't kill or steal."

"That's perspective," William said. "Would you feel pretty good about yourself if God had you stand next to Hitler?"

"Of course! I'd never do the awful things he did."

"Would you feel pretty good about yourself if you stood next to Jesus?"

I hesitated. "Well, um, you said he was and is God's son. I can't compete with that."

"Then, would it be safe to say that you're not as holy as Jesus?"

"Yeah, I guess so."

"Then, if you aren't as holy as Jesus, would it also be safe to say that you are a sinner?"

I pondered his words after William left. We continued through the book of John. On his fourth visit, William said, "David, would you like to be part of God's kingdom and experience the eternal life that Jesus offers?"

"Yes, I certainly would." By this time, I had no doubt that I qualified as a "sinner." Although I quit drugs the same day I left the Navy, I had continued with the heavy drinking.

"Let's pray together."

God, I know that I am a sinner, and sin separates me from you. I want Jesus to come into my heart and make it clean. I want to be free from drinking, free from porn. I want to be the man you expect and created me to be.

As I prayed to myself, and William prayed out loud, I felt the weight of my sinful ways melting away. I felt as pure and innocent as Matt the day he was born and knew that, at that moment, I was born into God's family.

"It would be a good idea to get into a church," William suggested. "You need to get around people who believe and follow Jesus. They can help you grow in your faith."

ൠൠൠ

The next four years passed in peace and harmony. I got a local delivery job which kept me home every night, attended church with my family and began participating in the church's music group.

"Hey there, handsome." The cute blonde let me in at the rear door to make my deliveries. My arm barely brushed her breasts as I passed by her. Old longings, feelings and emotions surged back. The rush of playing doctor with my girl cousins. The titillating shows at strip bars. Like a swimmer powerless against a riptide, I got sucked into the sea of lust again.

A touch here, a furtive feel there led to an unscrupulous sexual encounter. I knew better than to deny it. The Jesus in my life let me know I'd sinned — and hard.

"I really screwed up," I confessed to Kellie. My hands and voice shook as I related everything from childhood exploration to what I'd done that very day.

"If you want the other woman, have at it." She tried to stand tough, but I saw the pain in her eyes.

"I knew something was wrong," she finally sobbed. "I just figured it was partly my fault because of the how and why we married in the first place."

"Let's renew our vows," I suggested. "We'll make a fresh start."

જાજાજા

"We have a super youth program at our church," my friend Rich said in 1990. "Over at Ridgefield Nazarene. Come check it out. I'll bet Matt would love it."

"He's 14. I'm sure it would be good for him. What night do they meet?"

"Wednesdays."

"Okay, we'll be there next week."

When the youth leader found out I played guitar, he asked me to help lead the music for the youth group.

"Of course. I'd be honored."

REFUGE

"By the way, one Sunday a month, the youth lead the service for the congregation. You good with that?"

"Sure."

"Would you come to Ridgefield Nazarene to hear me play?" I asked Kellie the Sunday the youth were scheduled to lead the service.

"That would be nice."

We both attended services regularly after that. I worked hard to rebuild Kellie's trust, strengthen my family and grow as a believer in Jesus.

Four more years passed.

ॐॐॐ

I knocked on the back door of a restaurant, hand truck filled with the morning's deliveries. A beautiful brunette opened the door.

"Hey, handsome," she said as I passed by her. I dropped off the shipment and turned. Buxom Brunette stood smiling, her top completely unbuttoned.

Like a hapless salmon, lust hooked me and threw me into the boat of illicit desire again. I looked forward to our weekly rendezvous. I worshipped on Sunday and lusted for Tuesday. I allowed myself to lose control, and a simple touch turned from a thrilling moment into a tragedy.

"I got fired today," I told Kellie. I sat down with a thud while my breath came in bunches.

She turned from the kitchen sink. "*Fired?*"

"Yes." I worked my lips, but no sound came forth.

"You planning on telling me why?"

"Sexual harassment."

"Oh." I watched the light fade from her eyes.

"You ready to go to youth group soon?" Matt, then 18, walked in the kitchen.

I shook my head. "Not going tonight."

"Why?" He looked at me, trembling, and at his mother, weeping.

"What's going on?"

"I got fired today for sexual harassment."

He took a step back. "How could you do this to Mom? To me? You're no dad. You're disgusting. I never want to see you again."

The door slammed as he left — alone.

The hours passed.

I sat alone in the darkened living room, and I pondered the wreck of my own making. *My own stupid, selfish lust. Was it really worth destroying my family? My marriage?* I'd been so caught up in the rush that I'd never thought it through until that very moment.

A knock at the door startled — and shamed — me. *Whoever it is, they'll know I'm home. I have no choice but to open the door.*

Three leaders of the church stood on my porch. Before I could open my mouth — either in excuse or explanation — Pastor Mike held up one hand.

"David, before you say a word, we want you to know that we love you."

Say what? My mouth dropped open. I gasped for air.

"We love you, David. Can we come in?"

I stepped to one side as they filed in.

"You know we will have to remove you from the worship team, but that doesn't affect our love. We want you to know that we are behind you 100 percent and will help you win the victory over this struggle." Pastor Mike laid a hand on my shoulder. "We are all sinners saved by God's grace. We may struggle with different sins, but we all struggle, and it's all sin. Sin is sin. God doesn't think your sin worse than mine. It's all the same to him, and Jesus died to remove it all."

"We don't condemn you," one of the other leaders said. "We're here to offer you our support."

Although amazed by their kindness, shame kept me from Ridgefield. But, after three weeks, I couldn't take the isolation any longer.

"I can't stand it," I told Kellie. "I miss my church family. I have to go and face whatever is thrown at me."

"I'm going with you."

Kellie and I walked into the sanctuary together. We sat together. After Pastor Mike's message, he asked anyone who wanted prayer to come to the front. Kellie and I walked up the aisle together.

I stood with my head hung low and eyes squeezed shut as Pastor Mike prayed for me — for us.

"… we commit our brother and sister to you. In the name of Jesus we pray, amen." It seemed an eternity passed before Pastor Mike ended his prayer with arms open wide and a smile on his face. "Look, this is a sea of love." With great reluctance, I opened my eyes and turned around. Kellie and I gasped in shocked disbelief.

The entire church is standing — in solidarity — for us. Tears of shame and relief and healing tumbled down my cheeks. *I will do whatever it takes to overcome this weakness.*

Pastor Mike told me about a church that hosted a support group for Christian men like me, who struggled with sexual addictions. I was relieved to learn I wasn't alone in my weakness as the other men and I worked our way through an intense six-week course. We made ourselves accountable to one another, as well as to God.

❧ ❧ ❧

"For the grace of God that brings salvation has appeared to all men. It teaches us to say 'No' to ungodliness and worldly passions, and to live self-controlled, upright and godly lives in this present age" (Titus 2:11-12). I quoted this verse to myself every time women flirted with me and I flirted with past desires.

I got another driving job. Sometimes I felt so strong, like God rode in the cab of the truck with me. Other times I felt the old me wanting to prevail.

"If anyone is in Christ, he is a new creation; the old has gone, the new has come" (2 Corinthians 5:17). *Old David, you are dead. Now, I live in the reality of God's power, love and forgiveness.*

REFUGE

Eighteen months passed. Wins grew, and losses lessened.

"David, could you help on the worship team next Sunday?" Pastor Mike asked. "I've been watching you. I see true repentance. I see real growth."

"Thank you. As long as I rely on God's strength, and not my own, I'll make it."

And what of Matt, my son, who'd left home in disgust the night I revealed my deepest sin?

"I told Pastor Mike after youth group," he'd said that awful night. "He prayed with me and showed me how we are all sinners in one way or another. I'm sorry, Dad."

Then Matt had hugged me. "You've been a good example to me as a father and a man. Please forgive my harsh words. I love you, Dad."

I stood with the rest of the worship team that first Sunday back. Tears threatened to choke me as I looked out over the people standing before me. People who had loved me, accepted me *as is* and encouraged me as I fought my worst impulses.

One unit. One family. Serving one God.

That's Ridgefield Nazarene Church.

HIS LOST CHILDREN
The Story of Brandon and Janelle
Witten By Ameerah Collins

Brandon

The pungent odor of earthy smoke stained the air as I stumbled across the living room. My vision blurred, and I stretched out my arms, clinging to the wall to steady my balance. Piercing music pounded against my eardrums and seemed to infiltrate my brain and bounce around like a raging animal. Every chord, instrument and screech rained through my mind. I plopped face down on the sofa as my friends' raucous laughter filled the air.

"Brandon, dude."

They chortled at my expense while sitting around a small coffee table. I could hear them puffing on another blunt, passing it around and scolding one another for hogging it too long.

"You are really messed up, man," they teased when I declined any more hits.

You have no idea how messed up I really am, I nearly said.

Instead, I released a humorless chuckle. The lightheaded feelings of my marijuana-induced haze were finally starting to descend, but I wasn't sure if I really wanted those feelings to end or not. My nose rubbed against the cushion as my mom's pale and sickly face abruptly bombarded my mind. I silently cursed as gloom and rage crept back into my heart, thinking maybe I should have taken another hit after all.

What am I supposed to do without her? The thoughts filtered through my head and struck my gut with a heavy blow. Darkness consumed me as I struggled with feelings of loss, confusion and pure uncertainty. I was so angry. I hated that my life was falling to pieces, and trying to pick up those pieces was like scooping up handfuls of broken glass.

Memories of me driving my mother back and forth to the hospital for chemotherapy sessions skittered across my mind. For so long, I was just a kid caring for his dying mother. I could see myself pulling over to the curb, rubbing her back and holding her hair as she vomited on the side of the road. I recalled watching her for so many days and nights as chemo tormented her body. I could do nothing to ease her pain, nothing to take away the ache, nothing to put that beautiful smile back on her face. I felt so powerless.

But I found something to ease my pain. If only for a little while, I could be free from it all. I slowly sat up from my relaxed position and said, "Pass the blunt."

જ્જ્જ્

Throughout my childhood and early adolescent years, my mother was always the constant and prominent figure in my life. Though my father was at home, he didn't dedicate much time to his family. He was a Vietnam veteran, and I knew that had much to do with his withdrawn and distant nature. Unlike Mom, he didn't play with us outdoors, take us out for ice cream or just sit around and converse. While I grew up developing a special bond with Mom, my dad always seemed like a stranger in the house.

In 1993, doctors diagnosed my mother with cancer. I was 14 years old, my older siblings had since moved out of the house and the thought of losing my mom boggled my mind. Picturing a life without her was something I never wanted to imagine or experience. I couldn't live without her. I may have been a mama's boy to some, but I didn't mind it at all. Therefore, I made it my business to make Mom as comfortable as possible. I wanted to undo it all — any pain she felt, every heave of her weak stomach and each strand of hair she lost. If I could, I would have traded places with her.

When I turned 15, I began learning how to drive. My mother needed to get back and forth to her chemotherapy sessions at the hospital, and my dad wasn't always able to take her. Though it was hard witnessing my strong, smiling, courageous mother deteriorate into a weakened, fragile, exhausted state, I stepped up to the plate and cared for her just as she'd cared for me throughout my life.

"Brandon." Mom turned to me in the passenger seat of the car. We'd just come from one of her chemotherapy sessions, and this one had taken a toll on her. Her head lolled against the headrest as sweat glistened across her forehead. "I'm so nauseous, sweetheart ... and tired."

I looked over at Mom, my eyes narrowing in concern. Her head slumped over with an almost blank look on her face. "Do you feel like you have to throw up, Mom?"

She shrugged her shoulders and winced at the small movement. "Maybe," she barely whispered. "We should pull over, just in case."

I immediately pulled over to the curb and climbed out of the car. I rushed over to my mom's side as she clumsily propped the door open with her slim fingers and leaned out. I scooped her thin hair in my hands, pulling it from her face, and placed my palm on her back.

I crouched down beside her and leaned my head on her shoulder as I felt her quiet sobs shake her small body. I clenched my eyes shut, realizing how much more I could feel her spine this time — it seemed like she was getting tinier every day. She suffered through a few dry heaves before shaking her head in frustration.

"I don't think I have to —" Mom suddenly purged on the side of the road. The zooming of passing cars did nothing to silence the wretched sounds coming from my mother. A buildup of tears suddenly clouded my vision, and I rapidly blinked my eyes, willing the tears to disappear.

జ్ఞ్ఞ్ఞ

Janelle

Growing up, my father had a drinking problem — a problem that made him unusually grumpy and hard to please. And my mother, she worked so often I barely saw her. Throughout my childhood, I'd always been the good girl, while my older brother, Logan, was a bit of a wild card. I got good grades, studied hard and never gave my teachers any trouble. I was *that girl*, the seemingly perfect daughter. However, that wasn't enough to get my father to notice me or for my mother to cut back on work hours. And it wasn't enough for them to realize the longing I had on the inside from the lack of the affection, attention and love they were supposed to give me.

I was just a teenager when I started drinking every now and then. Logan would have a few friends over for drinks while my parents were out, and they'd include me every now and then. Drinking wasn't something I did on a regular basis; it was simply meant to take the edge off or to remind me that I wasn't as invisible as I felt.

"Janelle." Logan entered my room while I was studying for a test. He leaned against the wooden doorframe waiting for me to look up from my textbook. "Mom's working late, and Dad's out drinking with some buddies. I'm having a few friends over, all right?"

"Yeah, okay." I returned to my textbook. When my brother didn't leave, I looked back over to him with a raised eyebrow. "What's up?"

"Nothing, just …" Logan ran a hand through his hair and said, "I'm not trying to get all sentimental on you, but you've always got your head in those books. You should hang out with us more often. Lose yourself. Have fun. You don't have to be so perfect for Mom and Dad. It's not like they're here, anyway, ya know?"

"Why put in the effort at school if it doesn't even matter at home, huh?"

Logan sighed. "I didn't say all that, sis. I just want you to have a little fun."

I knew exactly what Logan was trying to say. Just like he'd gotten sick of my parents being away so much, I'd begun to get sick of it, too. I knew Logan never intended for me to stop caring about school when he told me to have a little fun, but as I joined him more often, I started caring less about textbooks and more about the next drink in my hand. A hollowness took root inside, causing me to feel empty and broken.

I knew I was a good student, that I had the potential to be a great daughter, but what was the use when my father was an alcoholic and my mother a workaholic? Drinking started as something to do at a social gathering or a way to kick back with friends — then it became my escape. I consumed drink after drink, trying to fill the emptiness I couldn't figure out how else to fill.

It was during this time that I met Brandon. He and Logan were friends, and Brandon usually came over to hang out. He was a musician, too. When I first saw him, something drew me to him. I knew he would be an important person to me. I knew would have a connection. It wasn't just because we both had difficulties at home or that I admired his passion for playing the guitar — it was something more. I just couldn't put my finger on it.

HIS LOST CHILDREN

❧❧❧

Brandon

In August 1995, doctors recommended my mother be placed in hospice care. I was visiting my older brother in Tennessee when we received a phone call from her nurse. They were expecting my mother to pass away soon and thought it would be best if my brother and I returned home to say goodbye. We booked a flight that same night, but we were 15 minutes too late. After my mother's funeral, everything else fell apart, too. I dropped out of high school, drinking became my new pastime and I eventually moved out of my childhood home.

I shifted from place to place for a while. I stayed with friends, a few family members and at one point I was even homeless. I was a 16-year-old high school dropout without a steady job, and I had no desire to become someone else's problem. Grieving over my mother proved too much for me to handle. I had no idea how to cope with the feelings of emptiness, loss and total abandonment. Then I experienced a new low.

My sister-in-law, Elena, and I visited my father's house to retrieve some of my mother's belongings. However, to our surprise, we found he'd put everything in the house up for sale. It didn't matter if the clothes, books, jewelry or furniture belonged to my mother or to me, my father wanted Elena and me to pay for whatever we wanted to take.

"I'm not paying for my own mother's things!" I

shouted in my father's face on the front lawn, not caring who heard our argument. "I don't have anything of Mom's. You can't just sell all her stuff without me having a say! What the heck is wrong with you?"

"If it's in my house, then it belongs to me!" my father yelled, his fists clenching at his sides as his nostrils flared and his face reddened with rage. "You don't live here anymore! You up and left, boy! You want something, you pay for it!"

"Whoa, whoa, whoa." Elena placed a hand on my shoulder and eyed my father. "This stuff doesn't just belong to your wife. Some of it belongs to Brandon, too. And there are letters from family members, pictures and photo albums, things from the funeral —"

"Shut up!" my father screamed at her. "If you want something, you pay for it. That's it!"

I left my father's home empty-handed, feeling utterly lost and alone in my own little agonizing world. I was so consumed with fury and misery that I smoked marijuana and tried a few other drugs with some friends of mine. Doing drugs was something I'd never really been into before that night. Alcohol was my thing, not drugs. But the feeling of being high provoked a numb sensation in me that I hadn't experienced before. The pain of not retrieving any of my mother's belongings slightly eased, and a dizzy calmness washed over me.

After a while, my high slowly began to come down. Images of my mother in her sickest moments flooded my mind. The anger and rage I felt toward my father bubbled up in my gut, making me feel the anguish I wanted so badly to escape. My mind fixated on the things I couldn't mend, and I decided I needed more drugs. When I asked my friend to pass me the blunt, the house phone suddenly rang, and he jumped up to answer it. It was my uncle.

"Brandon, I heard about what your father did. I'm so sorry, man," my uncle said. I heard the concern in his voice and could picture him rubbing his eyes as he spoke to me over the phone. "Where are you? I'm worried about you, kid. I haven't seen you in a while."

Hearing my uncle's weary voice provoked shame and regret in me. I hated that he was spending time worrying about me, while I was spending mine getting high.

"I'm fine," I told my uncle with a hard sniff. "I'm just hanging out at a friend's house. You don't have to worry about me. I'll be all right."

࿇࿇࿇

Janelle

In March 1997, Brandon and I started dating. We were 18 years old and were together for about three months before I decided I couldn't handle Brandon's lifestyle. Although I'd acted out in my earlier teenage years with the drinking and partying, I didn't agree with Brandon and his drastic drug and alcohol use.

In July, just a month after we broke up, I discovered I was pregnant. I was terrified about what Brandon would say. When I hunted him down at a party the following night, he freaked out. I stood there in the middle of a sea of dancing bodies, screeching girls and blaring music as Brandon shouted at me.

"How could this happen? Are you sure it's mine? I can't be a dad, Janelle! I can't do this!" He buried his face in the palms of his hands for a moment before shaking his head in disbelief. "No, I'm not doing this. I can't take care of a kid!"

I sneered at him in pure incredulity. "Did you really just ask me how could this happen? Am I sure that it's yours? What the heck do you think I am, Brandon?"

"That's not what I meant, and you know it!"

"It's exactly what you meant! And why can't you take responsibility for your part in this? I thought you were better than this!" I clutched at my abdomen, feeling sick to my stomach at his reaction. "You know what? I'm out of here."

Though I tried to remain tough during the argument with Brandon, as soon as I turned my back on him, tears welled up in my eyes. Although we weren't together, I wanted him to reach out to me. I silently begged him to call my name and apologize for hurting me and rejecting our child. I wanted him to change. I was willing to give up drinking and partying for the little one inside of me. I just couldn't understand why Brandon wasn't willing to do the same.

After Brandon's reaction, I feared approaching my parents with the news. My mother had always warned me she'd prefer me to ask her for birth control pills than to surprise her with a pregnancy. Thinking back on that conversation made me even more afraid to tell her.

The morning after contemplating how to tell my mother, I went to the bathroom and shuddered at the sight of blood. I wadded up more tissue paper and whimpered when more blood appeared. I didn't know anything about pregnancies and bleeding. I wasn't sure if the convenience store pregnancy test had been wrong and I was getting my period or if I was having a miscarriage. Scared and confused, I immediately rushed to my mother.

"Mom." I fidgeted with my hands as I leaned against the doorframe and watched her bustle around in the kitchen. "I have something to tell you."

My mother raised an eyebrow in my direction with a look of concern. She wiped her hands on a dishtowel and swung it over her shoulder. "What is it? Are you all right, honey?"

I shrugged my shoulders. "I don't know. I think I might be pregnant, but I'm bleeding." My mother's eyes widened as she clutched onto the kitchen counter for support. Before anything could come out of her mouth, I said, "I know it's bad, and I'm sorry, Mom. I just … I don't know if the bleeding is my period or if it's a miscarriage."

I bowed my head in disgrace as my mother covered her mouth with the palm of her hand. I knew she was in shock — in total disbelief that her nice and sweet daughter had gotten herself pregnant. I lifted my eyes to her when I heard her release a sigh. I watched as she stomped toward me, and then I lowered my eyes again.

REFUGE

"Be ready in the morning, Janelle. I'm taking you to the doctor's office. And you better hope it's your period and not a baby."

The spotting stopped, and a pregnancy test at the doctor's office confirmed my pregnancy. My mother was so angry with me. When my father found out, he didn't speak to me for a while. I was a disappointment to them, and I knew it. It took my father months before he could even talk to me about the baby. But after the shock finally wore off, my mother became my biggest supporter. She attended Lamaze classes, badmouthed Brandon when I told her of his reaction and went to doctor visits with me.

In March 1998, I gave birth to a little girl. Brandon came to the hospital when I was in labor. My mother hated him being there, but I felt differently. Mom didn't understand Brandon like I did. She didn't see what I saw in him. I knew where his terror of being a father stemmed from. It made me happy, knowing that he'd made an effort in the latter months of my pregnancy and came to the hospital to be present during the birth of his daughter.

I cautiously sat up in the hospital bed and eyed Brandon as he held our little Andrea in his arms. The wrinkles in his forehead and the slight narrowing of his eyebrows clearly showed his fear and a mix of concealed thrill. He cooed at her and hesitantly stroked her soft cheeks as if careful not to hurt her.

"I'm a father." He whispered it so low that I barely heard him. "I'm *your* father, and you're *my* baby. My Andrea." Brandon looked up at me then, and my breath caught in my throat when I noticed his eyes glistening with unshed tears. "I'm scared, but I'm also excited. I'm so sorry, Janelle. I'm going to be here. I'll try to be what you and Andrea need."

"I know," I said. "You're not alone, though. I'm scared, too."

Brandon and I didn't realize it at the moment, but Andrea saved our lives. Though we'd done so much wrong in our short lives, we believed it was God who had given us something special. My drinking and partying could have increased if I'd never gotten pregnant. Brandon may not have taken a second look at his life and realized he could benefit from change.

I can remember waking up in the middle of the night at the hospital and looking over to my side to see Andrea asleep in her little hospital bassinet. I sucked in a deep breath as the realization of being a mother finally hit me.

"I'll never be alone, and neither will you," I said. "You're my new beginning … and I thank God for you."

෨෨෨

Brandon

Andrea sparked change in me. I no longer desired to spend so much of my time smoking, drinking or partying with friends. Janelle and I got back together and decided to do our best to become a family. While she worked toward graduating from high school, I worked construction jobs. We eventually got our own place together, and it felt good knowing I was providing for my family. Up until then, it was my biggest accomplishment.

Janelle and I had our falling outs here and there, but we usually found our way back to one another. I wasn't as serious about the relationship as I should have been, and I still drank and partied more than Janelle liked. The last fight we ever had was our biggest, though.

Our relationship had been rocky for a while, and I decided to move back in with my dad. For three months, I bailed on Janelle and Andrea. It wasn't long before I started missing them. I realized exactly what I'd left behind when Janelle and I happened to attend the same wedding.

Janelle was the maid of honor, and I was the musician. Seeing Janelle made me really miss her and scold myself for leaving behind the best thing in my life. I tried my hardest to get her back. I'd corner her at the oddest times. Even during the rehearsal, I tried to sweet talk my way back into her life with promises, vows and heartfelt dedications. It was a conversation over the phone that finally did it, though.

"Brandon." Janelle sighed at the other end. I could hear sweet Andrea in the background, and just the sound of her tiny voice encouraged me to keep pushing Janelle to give me another chance. "I already told you this. I can't go through what I went through with you before. I understand you love your music, and you like to drink and stay out late. I get that. But that's not for me anymore. I have to think about Andrea now."

"I promise you I won't drink as much," I pleaded. "I've tried to live without you and Andrea, and I just can't. I'll put my family before my selfish needs. I'll be serious about us this time. I want to make you happy, Janelle. I want to be there for you and Andrea."

"I want more children, too," Janelle said with a leap of confidence in her voice. "I want a relationship that will develop and prosper. I want you to be around more, Brandon. If I let you back in my heart again, I can't take … I mean, you can't …"

"I know, Janelle. I won't hurt you. I promise I won't hurt you or Andrea."

Despite all the reasons for Janelle to push me away and reject my pleas and promises, she gave me another chance, and I was dead-set on not screwing it up. Janelle saw potential in me and decided to take a risk. She later told me that she felt a push to give me another chance. She believed it was God encouraging her to work things out with me.

I noticed Janelle had been referring to God more than usual, and it reminded me of my mother. She'd always say, "Jesus is always there and everywhere." It took me a while to finally realize what my mother meant. Jesus loved us. He knew our problems. And there was nothing he couldn't fix.

I moved back in with Janelle and Andrea, and I made sure I kept every promise I made to them. I stopped my alcohol usage and took our relationship seriously. Though I played music in bars and alcohol was free, I knew that if I took a sip it could compromise what I had going on at home. Janelle and Andrea were the most important people in my life, and I wanted it to stay that way. In September 2004, Janelle gave birth to our second daughter, Katerina, and just a few years later, we had our first son, Aaron.

కావా

Janelle

In 2008, we moved to Ridgefield, and Brandon and I started to feel something was missing in our lives. He'd finally landed a career job as a machinist, and I had the children I'd dreamed of having. Though we were content with our lives, we didn't feel whole or even secure.

In April 2010, I gave birth to our fourth child, Max. I thought he was going to make that empty feeling in me disappear, but it simply grew. It wasn't until our oldest daughter, Andrea, was in middle school that Brandon and I realized exactly what was missing in our life.

One day, Andrea came home from school with a black sharpie mark on her neck. It looked as if someone had flipped her hair up and drawn a dash across the middle of her neck. I watched as she settled down at the kitchen table, pulled a few papers from her backpack and pulled her hair to lie on the side of her shoulder.

"Andrea," I said as I walked behind her and Brandon followed. "What's that black mark on the back of your neck? Did someone put that there?"

"Oh!" Andrea chuckled and waved her hand as if the

mark meant nothing. "These kids at school were just playing this stupid game, 'Nazis and Jews.' If you're a Nazi, you go around and put a sharpie mark on the necks of kids who are the Jews. It means you're killing them."

"Oh, my God!" I shrieked and looked at Brandon. His mouth was agape, and his eyes widened at Andrea's nonchalant explanation. "That's horrible! Did you ask for that mark?"

"No." Andrea eyed me curiously, as if she didn't understand my horror. "I wasn't even playing the game. Some girl just ran up behind me, marked my neck and called me a Jew. I didn't think much of it. It's just a stupid game, Mom. Why are you so worked up about that?"

"They're making fun of the Holocaust, Andrea. Those kids — they're minimizing such a horrific occurrence in world history. Millions of Jews were killed during that time, separated from their families and treated like animals. To play that out in school is just wicked."

Brandon and I explained the horrors of the game to Andrea until she understood why the game was wrong. At that moment, we realized that Andrea wasn't receiving a good enough moral foundation at school, and Brandon and I evidently weren't teaching it to her at home. That night we decided to start looking for a church to attend.

One Sunday, we decided to attend Ridgefield Church of the Nazarene. The first day Brandon and I walked in with our kids, we arrived during an hour between the services, and lots of people were walking around talking and having friendly conversations. Brandon and I didn't know what to do, so I stopped a woman and asked for help. She simply grinned at us and took Brandon and me by our hands.

She led us all over the church, pointing out different areas and leading us toward different classrooms. She showed us rooms where our children would go to learn about God and introduced us to several people.

Throughout the service, I was in awe. The songs of praise to God were so uplifting and upbeat. It was the first time I was able to pay attention to an entire sermon without getting distracted, bored or sleepy. I just had this feeling of everything being right. The people had such love and admiration for Jesus; I'd never seen people so in love with God.

When Brandon and I gathered the kids and headed back to the car, I almost hesitated to ask him how he liked the service. I loved the church so much that I wanted to come back the following Sunday, but if Brandon didn't like it, I knew I would have to respect his wishes and go church hunting some more.

"So …" I said as we made our way onto the road and back to our home. "How did you like the service?"

"I was in awe." Brandon softly chuckled, as if he still couldn't believe what he'd just witnessed and experienced at the church. "There's so much love there. I've never had someone grab my hand and show me around the church like that woman did. What was her name? Maureen or something? Anyway, I've never felt the presence of God, love and welcome like we did in that church."

"I'm so happy you said that!" I breathed a sigh of relief and laughed. "I want to go back! I love that church so much! It's like you can actually see God in them. Isn't that amazing?"

Brandon and I attended the church for a few weeks, and though we were new to having a church family and being in such positive social gatherings, we decided to jump in headfirst and see what God had for us. I ended up volunteering for Vacation Bible School, and Brandon offered to play the guitar for the worship team sometimes.

It was amazing seeing God work in our hearts and teach us how to be more loving people, just like the folks at Ridgefield Church of the Nazarene. Brandon and I began reading our Bible more and praying together. We recognized how close to God the people at church were, and we wanted that same connection with God. Learning of the love of Jesus and realizing how his death on the cross made it possible for us to be with him forever really struck us. I knew he died for us and all, but I just never grasped how monumental it was.

Not only did our relationship with God strengthen, but our relationship with one another strengthened. Seeing Brandon's love for and trust in God just made me love him even more. I'd always been hesitant about marrying Brandon because of the rocky start we'd had, but now that I was striving to live for God and follow the teachings of Jesus, I knew it was time for us to get married.

It's funny, because so many situations tried to arise while Brandon and I grew closer to God. We were planning a wedding and working diligently in the church when our landlord suddenly told us we had three weeks to pack up and move. Before attending Ridgefield Church of the Nazarene and really giving our lives to God, Brandon and I would have worried ceaselessly about the move. But this time we didn't. We put everything in God's hands and asked him to handle this situation in our life.

We ended up having to cancel the venue we'd picked for the wedding because we could no longer afford it after moving expenses, and we still hadn't found a place to stay. But throughout all this, deciding to trust God gave us such peace. We knew everything would be all right if we just trusted in him. There was no use in us fretting over our situation when we knew God had already figured it out — we just hadn't learned his plan yet.

Days before our moving date, a member from the church told us about a house for rent. We moved in that same weekend. The following week, we had our wedding at Ridgefield Church of the Nazarene — and the pastor married us. Everything just seemed to fall into place. Brandon and I were so in awe of God. We hadn't realized he loved us so much that he would work out such a gigantic problem as if it were nothing.

In August 2012, my girls and I were baptized. Brandon and I dedicated Aaron and Max to God — we promised God that we would help our young ones grow up to be lovers of Jesus Christ, that we would keep them in the church and help them remain solid followers of God.

I stood in the pool behind Katerina as Brandon held

onto Andrea and dunked her into the pool. I watched him do the same for Katerina, and when it was my time, the pastor leaned me back into the water. When he brought me back up, I felt renewed and revived — like I was finally on the right path in life.

I could feel God working within me. His presence was palpable and took over my entire being. I felt the love Jesus poured out to me on the cross so many years before just so I could be in heaven with him one day. And in that moment, I felt so valuable, so loved and precious in the sight of my creator. During those many low moments of my life when I felt invisible, lonely and lost, God was always there, just waiting for me to open my heart to him. How could Brandon and I not have known how much God cherished us, his beloved children? How could we not have known we had such an incredible father in heaven?

After the baptism, I felt the love of Jesus coursing through my bones, and when I looked at Brandon, I knew he could feel it, too.

Throughout our childhood and adolescent years, we felt damaged and neglected by the ones we wanted to make us feel loved and worthy of warmth and affection. Although Brandon and I grew up and became responsible adults, the emotional bruises of our earlier years still rested heavily upon our hearts. And even though we wrapped our arms around our children and ensured they felt the love we hadn't always felt, deep down we continued to harbor so much hurt.

To my great joy, God washed all that pain away. He

carefully placed our broken pieces in his hands and put us back together. He silenced our wailing hearts and filled them with his absolute love. No longer were we his lost children — we were found and loved by the most perfect father. What better place to be?

THE FINAL ANSWER
THE STORY OF DANA AND JIM
WRITTEN BY ALEXINE GARCIA

It started like any other day. The dull pain of everything we were going through throbbed in the background of my mind. It was a nice sunny day, and I was thankful that I could at least enjoy that. I walked out to my car after work thinking about my kids and what I would put together for dinner. Before I got into my car, I saw a paper flapping in the breeze under my wipers. I thought it was an ad and nearly threw it away. But then I noticed handwriting on it, so I unfolded the paper.

"Jim, your wife has been seen all around town with another man."

❧ ❧ ❧

Dana

Six months before that note, I'd told him I wanted a divorce.

"I'm just not in love with you anymore. What don't you understand about that?" A phone conversation probably wasn't the best choice, but Jim was already in Washington working his new job. The way he treated me was not right, and he needed to know it.

"Dana, you don't know what you're saying. Things will be less stressful once you get here."

"No, Jim. I just can hardly stand you anymore." Just because he earned all the money in the house didn't make my work any less important. Our three kids demanded all of my attention, but he acted like the effort it took raising them was no big deal. I had no life outside of our home, and I hated it. My decision was final. No way would I change my mind.

"What about our kids? Do you think divorce is going to help them any?" he implored.

Our children would be fine. I would still be their mother. Plus, divorce would bring peace to their lives, I reasoned. They wouldn't have to hear us arguing all the time. All I wanted was to be with someone who could make me happy. I pressed the red button to disconnect and threw my cell phone onto the passenger seat. I wasn't going to talk to him if he wasn't even going to listen. I waited at the next stoplight and decided to call Courtney.

"He doesn't listen."

"I already told you what you should do."

"But he doesn't want a divorce."

"When you get down here, you need to find your own place and live your own life. Once he sees that you are serious, he will sign those papers."

"But, meanwhile, I'm going to have to deal with the arguing and begging me not to do this. You also forget that I don't have a job or any way to support myself."

"Yeah, but you just have to stick to it, and do what

makes you happy. And speaking of happy, Steven called Joey yesterday and talked for a long time. Their conversation wasn't any different than ours right now."

The thought of Steven brought a smirk to my face. He was handsome, and we always did get along in high school. "Oh, really," I said ruefully. "What does that have to do with me?"

"I don't have to spell things out for you, do I?"

I had already been texting Steven about a job. It wouldn't be hard to test the waters and see if what she suggested proved true.

ॐॐॐ

Before I knew it, the four of us were enjoying a few beers and a movie in Courtney's living room. First-date butterflies swam around in my stomach. My hands got clammy and cold with excitement. I looked sideways at Steven to see if he felt the same way. He took a sip of his beer and reached for another slice of pizza with his eyes fixed on the TV screen. The light from the screen moved across his face in the dark room. He looked over at me with a crooked smile and winked.

On the way home the next morning, my phone buzzed in the passenger seat with a text message. "Had a nice time last night." I put the phone back down with a smile. I'd only been in town for one day, and things were already looking up.

Being with Steven felt so refreshing. We didn't argue

about every little detail of our lives. He took me out to lunch and texted sweet things. We got to know each other more each day. He was going through issues with his wife, so he understood what I dealt with at home.

ભ~ભ~ભ~

Jim

It wasn't even a whole day before Dana left for Courtney's house. When Dana got an idea in her head, changing her mind was like trying to crack a safe. I knew my wife was stubborn, but deep down my insides burned at the thought of Courtney. I sat on the porch with my father and watched Dana drive off.

"What am I going to do, Dad? She wants a divorce."

"Well, there isn't too much you can do. You know how stubborn she is. You need to keep on living, and give this time to work itself out. A little time on your knees wouldn't hurt, either."

When 2 a.m. rolled around and she didn't come home, I knew she was serious about divorce. Courtney had her ways, and she was influencing my wife. I didn't get much sleep that night.

As the sun rose, I paced back and forth in the living room and looked through the blinds of the front window. I walked back to the kitchen and took a sip of my coffee. She walked in the front door with a nonchalant look on her face. Dana acted like she'd just come home from buying groceries. She didn't bother looking at me when she muttered good morning. I felt more sad than angry as

THE FINAL ANSWER

I watched her walk to the hallway. What I really wanted to do was grab her and hug her and maybe even kiss her. But instead I stood like a block of concrete with my coffee mug held up in my hand. "Good morning," I said sarcastically in the empty room.

It wasn't right for me to blame my wife's actions on someone else, but Courtney made me so mad. There wasn't one thing in particular that I could pinpoint about her. It was just her whole demeanor. To me, she had a shifty, unreliable way about her.

Dana's treatment wore me down like a chisel chipping away at a sculpture. Each night that she left, I felt another piece of our marriage break away. She acted so cold and hateful to me, I figured she was out with someone else.

∾∾∾

I gritted my teeth as her phone buzzed on the coffee table. I pretended not to notice as she snatched it up. The glow of the screen lit up her smiling face. She clicked the buttons and giggled to herself. When she got up to go to the restroom, she tucked the phone in her pocket. It was so obvious what she was doing right in front of my face.

The day I came home with the folded paper from under my windshield wipers, she denied the whole thing.

"Why would someone lie about this?" I could feel my face grow red and hot as I stared at her, demanding an answer.

"I don't know, but that has nothing to do with me."

REFUGE

"You're such a liar!" I shouted in her face. I knew I wasn't going to get any kind of honest answer from her, so I left the room and slammed the bedroom door. I wanted her to follow me and try to apologize.

Now that I'd confronted her, I wanted us to make up and put this behind us. Instead, she left again and didn't come back for a whole week.

When Dana was at home, she continued to guard her phone like an animal protective of its prey.

"What have you been doing behind my back?"

"What in the world do you mean?" she said, looking stunned.

"I know this divorce is about so much more."

"No, Jim. You're just too dumb to see that I'm not happy with you."

"Stop all the lies, and tell me the truth."

"I am ..."

"Tell me the truth, Dana!" I shouted. I could see her frantically searching for a lie to tell me. "The truth!"

"Yes. It's true," she said, looking away.

"I knew it. I knew it." I shook my head. I paced back and forth and looked back at her. "Who is it?" I waited and watched her face go white as she tried to get it out.

"Steven," she said in almost a whisper.

"Steven? Courtney's brother-in-law?" She nodded, and my head began to feel dizzy with anger. I realized I was holding my breath. "I knew Courtney had something to do with this. She's a no-good, lousy friend, do you realize that?"

"You're such an idiot, Jim. She's my friend, and she cares about me and what's good for me."

"Do you think that breaking up our family is good for you?"

"Jim, we're not happy, and you know it. I'm just pursuing something better."

I was shocked. Couldn't she see how wicked her friend was?

"I bet you she's the one who put that note on my car. Open your eyes. She's not your friend."

It might not make sense, but the more Dana acted this way, the more I wanted her back. Nothing I could do or say could make her change her mind. So, instead, I began to pray. I asked God to bring her home. I desperately begged him to fix our marriage. I'd grown up in a Christian home and always had a strong faith in God. But I'd never before chosen to turn to him and rely on him so much.

When Dana called the week before Christmas, I thought it was an answered prayer.

"Why don't we spend the holiday together?" she asked.

I tried not to sound overly eager. "Yeah, you know, that would probably be best. The kids and my dad would really like that." Maybe she was rethinking her other relationship.

It was nice spending Christmas like a family again. The kids opened their gifts and watched movies with their mom and dad in the same room. But when she went right back to Courtney's house the next day, I knew that I couldn't continue pretending things were okay.

"I don't know how much more I can take of this. You need to stop teetering on this fence top and make a decision. If you are going to stay in the house, then you are going to stop sleeping on the couch and start acting like my wife. Otherwise, it is better for all of us if you move out." She looked at me with a hard, expressionless gaze. Her eyes glazed over with indifference.

"I'll pack my stuff tomorrow. Courtney has a spare room I can stay in." My faith that God would fix our marriage didn't change when she made that choice.

෴෴෴

With all the tension building up between us over the next few weeks, getting away on a fishing trip just made sense. Dana's brother and dad picked me up before the sun rose. Kevin was more than just a brother-in-law to me, even more than just a friend. He helped me get through this divorce. As rumors flew through our small town about what Dana was doing and how it was my fault, Kevin encouraged me. "You just got to keep praying and doing the right thing," he'd say.

The silence of the lake and the gentle sway of the boat were exactly what I needed. It was nice out in the middle of the water not worrying about anything, or so I thought. Kevin put his rod down and became very serious. I looked over and caught him staring at me.

THE FINAL ANSWER

"There's something we have to tell you, Jim." He looked sideways at his dad, and he put his rod down, too, and sat on the stool at the head of the boat. "We want to be the ones to break this to you before you hear it from anyone else. Dana is working for Steven." I stood staring at him for a bit, trying to figure out if I heard right. "You're a good man, Jim, and you're going to make it through this. What you have to do is just trust in God. He will help you make the right decision. He'll give you the strength to do what's right for your kids."

It was that very day that I realized just how bad the situation had been. Perhaps up until then, I was not truly facing the problem. But I was ready to do my part. I started taking my children to church every Sunday. Each night as I lay in bed alone, I prayed to God with more fervor to fix my marriage.

The kids enjoyed Sunday school and learned so much. Each night, they prayed as well. They loved their mother so much and didn't like seeing her gone. My dad and I were in the kids' room tucking them in for bed.

"Dad, I want to pray for Mom," Ryan said.

"That's good, son, you should pray for her."

"Is it okay for me to pray for her to come home?" My heart ached at the innocence of his question. He didn't understand the full extent of the situation. I looked over at my dad. I was worried that perhaps God's plan didn't include my wife coming home. I didn't want my boy to be disappointed and lose faith.

"What do you think, Dad?" I asked my father.

REFUGE

"I think you can pray to God for whatever you want." His answer drove a jolt of hope through me. Deep down, I prayed for the same thing. Even more so, I prayed for Dana to realize how terrible her friend really was.

The next month, Dana was able to afford a place of her own with money from her new job. I guess she chose the apartment complex across the street to be close to the kids. I knew it wasn't me that kept her nearby. I could see her front door from our front window.

Just the thought that she and Steven may be together was enough to break my heart. Instead of giving up, I fell to my knees at the couch and prayed to God, "Please fix this mess. Please open her eyes to the mistake she is making. Show her the truth about these people she calls friends." I was a big ex-football player crying like a baby. But none of that mattered to me. I just wanted my wife back.

☙ ☙ ☙

Coaching my son's tee-ball team helped keep my mind off of our crumbling marriage. Meeting new people and hanging out with other dads also provided good stress relief. Once a week, the knot in my back loosened as I joked and laughed with other dads.

"You know, Jim, I have a friend who went through what you are facing," Ricky said. After the note on my car, others received emails about my marriage, and rumors flew from mouth to mouth. My personal business became the talk of our small town.

"Really? Did he get back with his wife?"

"No, he sure didn't. But he came out on top. He has a new family and kids now."

I took Derrick's number and was surprised at how open he was with me. His son was on the tee-ball team, too, and we saw each other once a week. He really did know what I was going through.

"I took your advice and got some help."

"Really? Man, that's great," Derrick said. "Where did you go?"

"I'm attending a divorce support group at a church."

"What church hosts that group?"

"Ridgefield Church of the Nazarene."

"That's my church," he said with a chuckle. "God has a sense of humor, doesn't he?"

He told me about his ex-wife and the similar issues he faced with her. She ended up leaving him and marrying the man she cheated with. I didn't want this to end up being my story, so I dug down even deeper in my faith. The outlook of our marriage was grim, but I just couldn't give up. I began taking my children to church with Derrick's family every Sunday. Derrick texted me Bible verses throughout the day, and his wife babysat our kids.

☙☙☙

REFUGE

Every day was a struggle to keep going forward. As if divorce wasn't enough, life threw me another curveball.

My phone rang, and a friend's name appeared on the screen.

"Hello," I answered.

"Jim, there's been a horrible accident here on the highway. I think I saw Kevin's truck smashed into a telephone pole." I jumped into my truck and went to the accident. I almost wish I hadn't arrived when I did. I contacted Dana and her father and broke the news to them. Holding Kevin's dad back from seeing the horrible crash site was the hardest thing I ever had to do. I held him tight, and we ended up sobbing together for our loss.

Even though we were going through a terrible storm, I was happy to have all three of our kids with me under one roof.

"Dad, we want to camp out in the living room," Ryan said, while jumping on the couch.

"That's fine with me." They ran to their rooms and grabbed their pillows and blankets.

Phillip spread his blankets next to his sister's and looked up at me. "Where's your pillow, Dad?"

"Oh, I didn't know I was invited."

"Yeah!" Jillian shouted. She brought a tub of popcorn from the kitchen.

I set up my pillow on the couch as the kids laughed and played while watching cartoons.

Sometime around midnight, the sugar seemed to seep

out of their system, and they settled down. Their eyes drooped even as they fought the sleep. They looked like a litter of puppies curled up next to each other. I clicked the lamp off and got comfortable on the couch closest to them. Out of the blue, Jillian said to me, "Dad, I really want Jesus in my heart like Ryan has."

My own heart beat wildly in my chest, but I wanted to make sure she understood what she was saying. "What do you mean, Jillian?"

"He has Jesus in his heart, and I want that."

I turned the lamp on and looked down at her. She crawled out from under her blanket and got on her knees and looked up at me. She looked so happy with a big smile on her face.

"Do you know what that means, Jillian?"

"Yeah, he will live in my heart."

"Are you ready to accept Christ in your life?"

"Yeah, I want to be like you and Ryan. Am I going to be able to feel him in there, like a tiny little person?"

"What the heck, Jillian?" Ryan said. "He's not a mouse. You're not going to feel him running around."

We all laughed together at the silly image.

"Jillian, I'm going to lead you in this prayer. I just want you to repeat this, and say it straight to God."

She closed her eyes and clasped her hands. "Okay, Dad."

"Dear God, I'm a sinner, and I need your help. I want to accept your forgiveness for all my sins. I accept your son, Jesus Christ, as Lord and Savior over my life. Amen."

She opened her eyes and looked up at me with such a sweet smile.

"Now you're going to have to listen for his voice and do your best to live a Christian life," I said.

"You need to read your Bible and learn how he wants you to live," Ryan explained.

Excitement and peace mingled inside of me. Even if my marriage was full of pain, it remained clear to me that God continued working for the good of our family. My wife hated me, and my children suffered because of it. However, two of my kids now knew Christ and, I believed, were promised an eternity with God in heaven. I couldn't be too sad as I fell asleep on the couch that night.

༄༄༄

Dana

The excitement of a new relationship slowly began to fade. It became hard for us to deal with two divorces and try to make each other happy. I'd started seeing Steven because I thought it would make me happy, but I still felt miserable. Even though I had to see him every day at work, I began spending less time at restaurants and hotel rooms with him. Eventually, our relationship fizzled.

Even though my affair was over, seeing Jim's name on my buzzing cell phone drove me crazy. He just wouldn't give up, and it was so irritating.

"What is it this time, Jim?"

"Hello to you, too. Listen, I don't have much time to

talk, but I want to run something by you. I have to go to Vegas for a convention with this new job. Will you go with me? I was thinking that when my work is done we could spend some time together. My dad will watch the kids."

My stomach churned with confusion. My first reaction was to laugh and hang up. But something about his offer was alluring. Even if he drove me nuts, even if his persistence wore me thin, the fact that he still loved me gave me a funny feeling I couldn't ignore. This was a big decision to make, and I was so unsure of what to do. I was no longer dating Steven, so that wasn't the issue. I'd made so many mistakes, and I really didn't know what Jim was thinking. Either way, I guessed this trip would be a chance to see if we could have fun and get along, something that seemed nearly impossible for us.

When I deplaned in Las Vegas, I actually felt nervous to see Jim, which I took as a good sign. However, that quickly faded. He smiled and hugged me the moment he saw me. He took my carryon from my shoulder.

"How was your flight?"

"It wasn't bad at all."

"Do you mind if we sit and talk for a bit?"

"I haven't even been here two minutes and you're going to get heavy on me?"

"It's important." The beckoning look on his face tied my stomach into knots. I wanted to have a lighthearted weekend with him, but it looked like that wasn't going to happen.

REFUGE

We sat down in a coffee shop near the airport exit.

"I'm going to just get to the point with you, Dana." He paused and leaned across the table. "If we are even going to do this, I need to set some things straight. If you are going to take our relationship seriously, I need you to commit. You're going to have to quit that job, stop all contact with Steven and leave your apartment and come home."

I felt like my world was collapsing around me. Committing to him was one thing. But what he proposed took away all of my freedom. I felt like he was pulling a rug out from under me and leaving me face up on the floor. I'd be stuck at home with an allowance, all the housework, caring for the kids and unappreciated. I suppose my face revealed my thoughts because he didn't even let me talk.

"This is what I need from you if we are even going to enjoy this weekend."

"I don't think I can commit to quitting my job. I won't be able to support myself." Anger began to flow through me like a hot surge.

"I don't believe you, Dana. Are you really willing to throw everything away?" I could see the anxiety welling in his eyes. He needed me to say these words if we were even going to start this trip. I wanted things to work between us, but I felt the cycle starting all over again. I felt him sucking away my freedom.

My heart quickly snapped shut, and I began shouting, "I just don't know how you can sit here so pompous and demand me to change my entire life. And you want me to just blink and make this decision right here, right this moment."

"I just want to see you commit to me and your family. But it's obvious that that is not going to happen. From here on out, you need to keep your distance. You are not welcome in my home anymore. We will co-parent our kids, but that will be the extent of our relationship. For now, I'm catching a plane home."

I watched him walk away.

ৡৡৡ

Jim

I watched the expression on her face, and her feelings showed in her eyes. Something inside of me snapped. As she yelled in my face, a stern resolve of peace rolled over me, and I remained calm. My mind made up, I finally handed it all over to God.

"I just want to see you commit to me and your family. But it's obvious that that is not going to happen. From here on out, you need to keep your distance. You are not welcome in my home anymore. We will co-parent our kids, but that will be the extent of our relationship. For now, I'm catching a plane home."

It wasn't even hot anger that compelled me to get up and walk away. I just knew this was exactly how it needed to be. The desire to wrap my arms around her and keep her as my wife did not leave me. But I knew that wasn't going to happen. Now I could move forward in grieving our divorce and trying to start healing. Now she could go and live the independent life she wanted.

"How did it go?" Derrick asked.

I held the phone against my ear with my shoulder as I moved around the hotel room gathering my stuff. "Not good. I changed my flight home to tomorrow morning."

"I'm sorry to hear that. What happened?"

"Well, I laid it out like we discussed, and she turned me down. She's still more concerned about her own life than our family."

"And how are you taking this?"

"You know what? Surprisingly, I'm okay. I really think I'm ready to accept this and move forward."

"That's the power of prayer. Sometimes we don't always understand how or why God does the things he does, but he has a perfect plan."

I believed Derrick was right. I believed God's hands were all over this. There was no way that I could be so calm and so accepting of the way things turned out without his Holy Spirit guiding me. If I were going through this all alone, I would have been a crying mess.

I didn't hear from Dana until the next day.

"Where are you?" the text read.

"I'm on a plane home," I responded. This time my mind was made up, just like Dana's had been all along. I knew this was final as I turned the divorce papers in to my lawyer.

THE FINAL ANSWER

❧❧❧

Dana

His text felt like a sucker punch to the throat. I knew he was angry, but I didn't think he would leave me completely hanging in Las Vegas. I sat down in the hotel lobby stunned. *Should I change my flight, too? What the heck was he thinking leaving me all alone?* It was in this moment that that icy spot inside of me began to slowly melt. I could feel my cold heart start to drip. A tiny whisper entered my mind: *You are wrong.* The sight of Jim walking through the airport doors came back to mind. *How in the world did things get this bad? Jim probably thought I didn't want to commit to him. Even worse, maybe he thought I still wanted to be with Steven.* I'd made so many mistakes, I even wondered if he really could take me back.

I decided to stay in Vegas for the next few days. A vacation couldn't hurt. But the colorful shows, the bright lights and all the fancy restaurants weren't much fun alone. The whisper did not fade. It actually grew louder. Several other thoughts and questions came to mind, too. *Is having my own life worth all this heartache? I am missing out on special moments with my family because I want independence. My kids spend half the week without me. Even after all that I have done, Jim is willing to take me back? But wait. Would he?* Something in his face was different at this last meeting. He seemed more stoic and adamant. The quiet begging in his eyes had left. I started to panic. Up until then, I had a hold on him. I knew I could go back home if I really wanted. But I had a feeling things were going to be different.

I believed that it was God's voice whispering, *You are wrong.* All that time, I was pushing away the truth. I'd stopped going to church because I knew I couldn't go to church and pretend to be a Christian and live this horrible life at the same time. All along, I lied to myself about my relationship with Steven by justifying my actions. I listened to the wrong advice from the wrong friends and ignored God's voice.

Then the worst thing that could happen did. Courtney's boyfriend ended up visiting Jim. He told him everything. Jim found out exactly what I'd been doing and everything I'd lied about.

The day I wrote that note, I never really thought about the outcome. All I was thinking about was my own happiness. As I scribbled, "Jim, your wife has been seen all around town with another man," I just wanted him out of my life. I never imagined how hurt he would be if he found out it was me who wrote the note.

My world crumbled at that point. My friends betrayed me. Everything Jim tried to warn me about was true, and my family didn't even want me in their home. I couldn't go on denying what I had done. Each day, the weight grew heavier, and I didn't know what to do about it.

I showed up at Jim's house on a Sunday afternoon, glad to find him sitting on the porch.

"Hi," I called out from the driveway. He gave me a

cordial wave. "I just need a minute of your time." He came down to the driveway.

"What's up?"

I did my best to remain composed, but I could feel my insides quivering. "Listen, I just want you to know that I am sorry about everything I have done and everything I put you through." He stood towering over me with his arms crossed and anger written on his face.

"Well, thank you for that," he said.

I was stunned. This was not the reaction I was expecting at all. "Well, I guess that's it."

I was really hoping he'd say something else or invite me in to talk.

"All right then," he said.

I drove away bewildered. Even though his reaction was not what I hoped for, the heavy weight of guilt began to lift. I felt each bit of shame wipe away as I apologized to God as well. It felt good to be free of it all, but I still wanted my family back. I found myself praying to God every day. I asked him for help, for a miracle even.

I couldn't stand being away any longer. I showed up at Jim's house and was greeted by my kids. I was surprised when they let me in.

"Wait here, Mom. I'll go get him," Jillian said with a huge smile. It gave me some satisfaction that she was so eager to see me. He left me waiting for quite a while. I suddenly wondered if maybe he was blowing me off. I figured he must want me to let myself out, and tears began to flow. My last hope started fading. Then he walked in the room, and I felt so relieved to see him, even if he looked disappointed to see me.

"Let's go to the back room. I don't want the kids to see you like this." He walked to the back of the house, and I followed. We sat down on two couches opposite each other.

"What's going on, Dana? I thought we talked enough the other day."

"I'm just so sorry. I'm sorry about every single lie and every single wrong thing I have done to you. I know that the divorce is about to be final, but I really am sorry. I don't know if you will take me back, but I will spend the rest of my time fighting for you and the kids. I love you." At this point my eyes were bloodshot, and I was sobbing. I was vulnerable in front of him, but it didn't matter.

"I just wish you would have come and talked to me before the divorce papers went through." He looked at me long and hard, and his hard expression melted into kindness. Right in that moment, it felt as if God unfolded his hand and answered every single prayer that each one of us had sent up to his ears.

"I forgive you," he said. My heart thumped, and I let out a laugh of relief. It wasn't over just yet, though. I spent the next few hours telling the truth about everything.

My husband and children welcomed me back into their home, and we moved forward. As if having my family weren't enough, there was a mistake with the filing of our divorce papers, and Jim's lawyer went on a five-week vacation. Because she didn't respond and fix the problem, our divorce was not valid. It looked like a miracle to us, more evidence of God's hand moving in our lives.

During our time apart, I had gotten a job and supported myself. Jim took care of the kids and all the housework. Because of this, we each gained a deeper understanding for what the other went through on a daily basis. Even though I'd put my family through so much, we learned from our mistakes and came together in a new way. It was time for me to join my family in one more thing — the amazing faith they now shared.

The thought of returning to church scared me. All of Jim's friends knew everything I'd done because they were the ones supporting him through the heartache I'd caused. My palms got cold and clammy the first time I met his closest friends, Derrick and Amber. Amber had been babysitting our kids while Jim worked. When we arrived to pick them up, she greeted us with a warm smile.

"It's so good to meet you," she said. I searched her bright blue eyes for sarcasm but saw only sincerity. She invited us in and helped the kids pick up toys as we made small talk. Back at the front door, I was anxious to leave. Part of me wanted to bolt.

"Why don't you come back sometime so we can get to know each other?"

Could this woman really be this nice? Is this for real?

"Sure," I said with a slight smile. "That would be nice."

I began to think she was serious when she called me the next week. The funny thing was, she was sincere, and her intentions were honest. Instead of creating some fake friendship, she got straight to the point. "How are you two adjusting?"

I was a little startled by her bluntness, but I figured I could talk openly since she already knew everything that happened.

"We're getting along. We still argue, and we are far from back to normal, but we talk more now. He asks me questions about my time away, and I tell him the truth. It's not easy, but we are getting there."

"It will take time. I'm glad to hear you are doing well, though. Are you guys praying together?"

"Not really. The kids are really good at saying prayers at bedtime. They tell me that God brought me home because they prayed. Jim gives them Bible lessons from time to time. I'm just not really sure how to get back into it."

"You know, the best thing to do is to just jump right back in. Why don't you join us for church this weekend?"

It was amazing to see just how welcoming she was. I could hardly believe that she didn't judge me or see me as a horrible person. That Sunday, I accepted her offer and attended Ridgefield Church of the Nazarene. The people I met at church acted warm, just like her. They welcomed me like a new friend, not a cheating wife. The forgiveness that I received from God came from these people as well. When I sat down in church, I laughed to myself at the irony of the sermon. The pastor taught on the prodigal son — the one who left home, behaved in wild and selfish ways, only to be welcomed with joy by his father when he returned home. I figured God's sense of humor must be behind this. I felt him telling me that I was home now and that he was welcoming me with open arms.

❧❧❧

The hardest part has been accepting all the moments that I missed. While I was away, my kids were learning about Christ. They were reading the Bible and praying earnestly. They were even praying for me after what I had done. All that time, I thought the final answer to our marriage was my own choice. I came to realize that, in the end, God had the final answer.

The biggest moment that I missed was Jillian accepting Christ. My whole family was gathered around, and I was not there. But one beautiful Easter morning, she got baptized. Baptism is a public display of faith, but hers represented more than that. It was a public display that our family was back together and that God held us tight. She looked so beautiful on the stage in her frilly dress with ribbons in her hair. I'd never seen her smile so big. I looked up at Jim, and he looked down and squeezed my hand. His eyes were brimming and his smile infectious.

I thought of everything God has done for me, everything he has forgiven, everything in my life and my family that he's healed and helped make new.

REFUGE

Jillian stepped up to the microphone, her face radiating the beauty and innocence of her faith. I watched with joy and gratitude as my daughter addressed a coliseum full of people and told them, "I love Jesus."

I love Jesus. And he loves me, with open arms.

SEARCHING FOR PURPOSE
The Story of Grace

Written by Onyih Odunze

I'm ready, I thought as I stood in the hallway and stared at the garage door. The weight of sadness I had carried around with me for so many years would finally be lifted.

I desperately wanted freedom.

The rental was quiet — almost eerily so — and in the midst of my angst, I found time to wonder why. At least one of my four roommates was usually home at that time of the day. It felt strange to come home to an empty place, but perhaps this meant things were finally falling into place.

In order to kill myself, I needed to hurry before someone came home.

The silence wrapped around me, oppressive and stifling. I stood motionless, staring at the door that led to our garage. I imagined sitting in my white Chevy Impala, parked behind the door that stood in the way of my freedom. I would cuddle in the backseat with my beloved dog as we inhaled the life-ending fumes from the car exhaust.

Will it be painful? I wondered.

I didn't care about myself, but the thought of hurting my dog cut me to the quick. How could I hurt my loyal little friend, who loved me and depended on me to take care of her?

The desire to kill myself warred with a deep reluctance to hurt Hailey. I didn't want to leave her behind, but could I end her life as willingly as I planned to end mine?

❧ ❧ ❧

I was born in California in 1973. I suspected from an early age that something wasn't quite right with my family. My younger brother, Ben, and I lived with our parents in the suburbs of Napa at the Northeastern cusp of San Francisco Bay.

My brother and I were not close, so we never discussed such things, but we both knew about the arguments. My parents tried to hide them from us, but children are very perceptive, and we picked up on them.

Sometimes, all I heard were whispers behind the walls, arguments cut short the moment one of us children came within earshot. But it was enough to make me restless.

By the time I was 11, I'd found a way to escape the tension in our family.

"Where are you off to?" Dad asked.

"Oh, just going to a friend's house to hang out. I'll be back later."

My "later" sometimes turned into days, but if it raised any eyebrows around my house, my parents didn't let on. I think my father let me run free, hoping that might quiet the restlessness he sensed churning inside me.

I only grew more emotionally distant. My parents tried another approach. They started sending me to a string of counselors. We didn't talk much in our family, and I didn't find it much easier to confide in the counselors. This made it difficult for anyone to figure out what was wrong with me.

I sat on beige couches and stared at diploma-studded walls while they poked and prodded with questions.

"So, how are you doing, Grace?"

"Fine."

"Is there anything you would like to share with me today?"

"Umm … not really."

It was difficult to talk to them, and I never tried very hard. When things didn't pan out with one counselor, my parents found another one. The cycle went on for about four years — then my parents got divorced.

The quiet tension finally gave way to open disputes, and just like that, my parents' marriage was over, and my life changed forever.

᪥᪥᪥

"But, Robert, why send her so far away?" my mother asked.

"This school is really good. They have a great reputation for working with troubled youth, and I think that's what she needs right now."

My mother didn't put up much of a fight about my father's idea to send me to Italy because I don't think she had any idea what to do with me. Mom seemed always shrouded in an air of despair that contributed to the difficulties in our relationship. In addition, the divorce from my father had left her with a lot of residual bitterness, and she probably didn't mind the extra expense he was taking on by sending me to a boarding school in Europe.

And so I left home at the ripe age of 16 and went to Italy. The therapeutic boarding school adhered to the principle of teaching by example and the premise that behavioral modification could be achieved through peer and counselor modeling of desired behaviors.

Nestled on a steep hill on the banks of the River Arno in the Tuscany region of Italy, Arezzo was a different experience for me. The town was divided into two sections — the upper part and the lower part. The cathedral and the town hall were located in the upper part of Arezzo, and major streets branched off from there to the lower part. The buildings in the upper part lent the city a medieval appearance and gave one the feeling of being part of some grand old adventure.

Our days were tightly scheduled and filled with peer and group counseling sessions. In direct contrast to the uncomfortable counseling sessions I had endured in California, these sessions felt positive and uplifting. I don't know if it was being around other kids like me — flawed, broken and searching for something missing from our lives. Maybe it was the fact that the counselors who ran the school were firm but kind — it was easy to tell that they cared about us and really wanted to help us. Or, maybe it was a combination of several factors.

Whatever it was, it worked for me. In Arezzo, I learned to take ownership of my life and my issues. Even though the sessions helped change my attitude and steer my life in a more positive direction, I still was not diagnosed or taught how to manage my deep melancholy.

This lack would cause problems later in my life.

Besides moving my life in a different direction, I also made some good friends in Arezzo.

The best of them was Aidan. Aidan and I were both emotionally troubled, but for completely different reasons. Aidan came from the slums of Ireland and had several brothers who were heroin addicts. He was very quiet, more of an introvert really, and I knew he didn't like talking about his brothers or the mistreatment he suffered at the hands of his mother.

We kept our conversations light.

"What I wouldn't give for a Big Mac and fries," I would groan to Aidan and my other friends, a teasing note in my voice.

He always smiled in that quiet way of his. "You know there are no fast-food restaurants in Arezzo. The Italians don't go for that."

The Irish lilt in his voice made everything that came out of his mouth sound musical.

The fading sunlight sent shafts of soft light through the kitchen window, highlighting the reddish streaks in Aidan's brown hair, as he smiled his quiet smile.

REFUGE

We often went to the kitchen in the evenings at the end of our normal school day. Free time was very difficult to come by, and we spent what little we had gathered around a small table in the school kitchen, drinking tea and cracking jokes.

The conversations were lighthearted and carefree, a respite from facing our emotional difficulties.

Those evenings in the kitchen were some of the happiest times of my life.

❧❧❧

After spending about two years in Arezzo, Italy, I returned home to California to finish high school.

Even though I'd made progress at school, I still felt something missing in my life. I started looking for love, for acceptance, for the sense of belonging that I didn't have with my family. I got close to a boy in my school. Our friendship led to physical intimacy, and a few months later, I found out I was pregnant.

Eighteen years old, in my last year of high school and pregnant!

What on earth am I going to do?

After my parents' divorce, I shuttled back and forth between both parents and was living with my mother when I first got pregnant.

"You should have an abortion," she said when I told her what happened.

Shocked, I gasped. "No, Mom. I'm not having an abortion."

I knew in my heart that I could never abort my baby. I already knew what I wanted to do.

"Mom, I'm going to have the baby and put it up for adoption. I'm going to do an open adoption." In an open adoption, the birth mother and adoptive parents are allowed to exchange information before, during and after the adoption process. Choosing that option left the door open for me to have a relationship with my child.

I watched my mother and saw something crumble within her, almost as if the walls she constructed over so many years were finally coming down. Tears pooled in her eyes, and she looked at me with such despair that I was taken aback.

"No, Grace! Not adoption."

The depth of her reaction surprised me. Our family didn't get emotional. It wasn't the way we did things. I waited and wondered at the ferocity of her reaction. It seemed like ages before she spoke again. "I think putting a baby up for adoption is a very difficult thing to do. You would have to carry the baby for nine months … bond with it during that time. Giving it up may be very difficult."

She paused for a moment and looked at me.

"Are you sure you can handle that, Grace?"

I nodded my head, determined. "Yes, Mom. I've given it a lot of thought, and it's what I want."

When she saw that I wouldn't budge from my decision, she gave up trying to convince me, and then we told my father.

REFUGE

My father didn't react much. I knew he was a little disappointed, but he supported me from the beginning.

"We'll get through this together, Grace. I'm here for you … always."

A rush of gratitude welled up in me. "Thank you, Dad."

౿౿౿

Somehow, my father found a place for me to live while I was pregnant. It was a home for unwed mothers close to where we lived in the Napa Valley, and it was run by two middle-aged sisters.

"They'll take care of you here, Grace." My father's voice held a note of optimism as we drove up to the lovely Victorian home.

Unsure and a little scared, I nodded. "Okay, Dad."

He patted my hand, and the gesture reassured me.

"It's only until you have the baby. It won't be too long, you'll see."

I only stayed there a month.

There were four other girls living at the home when I arrived. Even though it was a big building, it only had five bedrooms, and we had to share because one of the sisters had a 16-year-old daughter who also lived in the house.

They often left the daughter in charge of us unwed mothers, and it was strange to hear her issuing orders to the rest of us, several older than her.

"These are your chores for today, Grace," she would announce, relishing her role as our *de facto* caretaker.

SEARCHING FOR PURPOSE

I didn't like it there, and the counseling sessions were no good, either. I'd seen a lot of counselors, both as a pre-teen and during the years I spent in Italy, and I had never encountered the kind of counseling they practiced at the home. The sessions seemed more focused on making us feel guilty for being pregnant than on any desire to help us.

After a month, I went home and lived with my mother for the rest of the pregnancy. I stuck with my desire for an open adoption, and I felt comfortable with the young couple I chose to raise my child.

In March of 1992, I gave birth to a healthy baby boy and handed him over to his new family. I knew I was doing the best thing for him — I was only 18, barely out of high school and with no resources to care for an infant.

I knew all that in my head, but my heart still gave a faint tug as I gave up all maternal rights to my son.

Oddly enough, as the years went by, I ended up developing a really great relationship with my son's adoptive mother, but I have never been able to form a relationship with my son, who as he grew up struggled with addiction.

❧❧❧

Later in 1992, I moved to Providence, Rhode Island, to attend college — a refreshing change and welcome distance from my family.

While there, I met a young man. We grew close, and our friendship progressed into a sexual relationship.

REFUGE

As luck would have it, I got pregnant. Again. I was in my first year of college and pregnant for a second time, barely a year after having my first child.

I could hardly believe it. *How did I let this happen?*

It never occurred to me that my lifelong search for love was leading me toward self-destructive choices.

This time, I took a different approach to the situation.

"I'm keeping my child," I told Bradley, my boyfriend at the time and the father of my baby.

"How are you going to take care of it?"

I stayed calm and tried to reason with him. "I can get a job. You don't have to be involved if you don't want to be. This is entirely my decision."

He gritted his teeth in frustration. "Well, it better be your decision because I'm out."

And he was. I didn't see much of him after that.

Unlike my first pregnancy when I decided on adoption right from the beginning, I was determined to keep this second child. As the long months of pregnancy dragged by, I grew more attached to and possessive of the baby.

I often talked to the child I was carrying, imagining what life would be like as a single mother. It seemed a daunting task, but I felt sure I could do it.

"I'll take care of you, baby. I promise," I whispered one night as I rubbed my swollen belly.

I was seven months pregnant when I realized that I couldn't keep my son. It finally dawned on me: I was still in my first year of college, with very few marketable skills and little or no support from my family.

SEARCHING FOR PURPOSE

How on earth would I be able to care for an infant all by myself?

I decided to put him up for adoption. The decision devastated me, quite unlike the first time.

The final months of the pregnancy and the adoption process itself were a very painful time for me. Again, I chose an open adoption because it would give me the opportunity to stay in my child's life.

My second son was born in May 1994. This time, when I handed him over to his new family, I felt my heart rip into pieces.

࿐࿐࿐

I felt lost and wretched for a decade after my second son's birth.

I moved from one city to another, living selfishly, somehow unable to form a lasting relationship. Searching, always searching for that place, that man, that thing that would finally complete me.

What am I doing here? I often wondered to myself. *What is the purpose for my life?*

I thought the "greater purpose" was to find a man, get married and have children. Surely, that would fill the gaping hole that yawned in my heart.

I didn't feel whole unless I had a man in my life. Nothing else mattered as long as I was in a relationship, and I did everything I could to make them last.

They never did. Not one of them did.

But I could never forget about one special relationship. Even though he was a boy when I knew him, I'd never forgotten Aidan — the red highlights in his brown hair, his smile, his quiet charm.

Due to the strict rules at our boarding school, Aidan and I were never anything more than friends. The school permitted no dating, so instead we'd developed a brother-sister kind of relationship.

In my heart, though, I knew I'd felt something different for Aidan. He was damaged, as I was. Maybe that was the bond that held us together, I'm not sure. But I loved him on a level deeper than my feelings for any other man.

We'd stayed in touch after I left school, writing letters back and forth, but I hadn't heard from him in a few years.

One day I said to myself, *Maybe I should go to Dublin and see Aidan.*

Traveling to Ireland seemed like an outlandish idea at first, but the longer I thought about it, the more merit it held. I had other friends in Dublin besides Aidan, and I figured it would be nice to see them all. I decided to surprise my friends, so I kept my plans a secret.

In August 2001, my father and I traveled to Ireland together. Once we got there, he made his own plans, and I was on my own for a week.

Before going to see Aidan, I decided to visit Colin, one of my former counselors from Arezzo, Italy. I knew he'd been working at a home for boys, and I looked it up in the phonebook and tracked him there.

Unfortunately, he didn't work there anymore, but everyone remembered him, and they gave me the address for his new office. I found him at another home for young boys who struggled with addictions, depression and other emotional issues.

His face lit up with delight when he saw me, and he enveloped me in a big hug.

"Hey, Grace! What are you doing here? Come to see us, have you?" His thick Irish brogue woke nostalgic feelings in me, and I laughed and hugged him back. Colin had been one of my favorite counselors, and I felt very comfortable around him.

We chatted back and forth, catching up with what was going on in each other's lives. After his initial joyful greeting, a hint of reserve crept into his manner, and I had a feeling there was something he wanted to tell me.

After 10 minutes of casual conversation, he turned serious. "Do you know about Aidan?"

The grave look on his face sent my nerves skittering. "No. What about him?"

My heart sank at the look in Colin's eyes. I knew how troubled Aidan was, and I was scared to hear the next words out of Colin's mouth.

Colin looked at me with grief and regret in his eyes.

"Grace, I'm not sure how to tell you this — but Aidan killed himself last year."

I sputtered in shock as my heart fell. I could feel the sting of tears pooling behind my eyes.

"What?" *Aidan … oh, Aidan. Why did you do it?*

Colin shook his head, grief stamped on his face. "Grace, you know what Aidan was like. How damaged he was."

I nodded. Yes. I knew how much pain Aidan lived with. He always wanted a better life, but found it so difficult to trust anyone — even those who were trying to help him.

Still in shock from Colin's news, I struggled to carry on the conversation. "Yes," I said slowly. "It almost seems like it was inevitable, with the way he was."

Colin continued. "The signs were right there, just before it happened. And me, a trained counselor, couldn't see them!" He ran his hand through his hair, disheveling his locks. "I should have seen it coming. I … I could have done something to save him," he sighed.

I shook my head. *I'm not sure anyone could have saved Aidan.*

Colin shared a few more details with me: how Aidan killed himself and how Aidan was doing before it happened.

"Grace, I was just about to leave. I live pretty far from here, so why don't we grab some dinner and talk some more. There's a restaurant close by."

So we walked over to the restaurant, ate some dinner and talked about Aidan. I could have eaten chaff for all I knew. Everything else paled in comparison to our loss — to my loss.

My mini-reunion with Colin was bittersweet. Of everyone in the world, Colin and I probably knew Aidan better than anyone else. We shared our happy memories of him and also talked about what had happened to him.

The more we talked, the more real it became. Aidan was gone. I would never see him smile again, never talk to him, never find out whether we were meant for each other or not.

I mourned Aidan's death, not just for what he meant to me in the past, but for the future we would never have.

Still consumed by thoughts of my dear childhood friend, I tripped on air on our way out of the restaurant and fell right there on the street. Colin and I laughed about it later — how could I have stumbled and fallen when there was absolutely no obstacle in my way?

The rest of my time in Ireland was a blur. The excitement of my trip disappeared, leaving shock and sorrow in its place. All I wanted to do was go back home.

My sorrow over Aidan morphed into an obsession. I became obsessed with understanding suicide.

I embarked on a lifelong research project toward understanding it.

෯෯෯

In spite of my selfish lifestyle and string of sexual relationships, I also went to church regularly. I longed for intimacy, and although I sometimes sought it in fleeting relationships, I was idealistic about marriage, and I believed it should last forever. I didn't want to end up divorced, so I waited a long time to get married.

REFUGE

I met Bryan at church, which I took as a sign that we shared the same ideas about marriage and faithfulness. I looked forward to a lifetime of happiness with him.

Bryan and I married in December 2004.

"I, Grace, take you, Bryan, to be my husband." I spoke my vows with confidence, certain that Bryan and I would be together forever.

"I, Bryan, take you, Grace, to be my wife."

My heart sang when we joined together as husband and wife, and I faced the future with optimism.

Finally, I'd achieved one of my lifelong goals. I was married. Now, it was time to face the other one — having children.

I was desperate to have children, and Bryan and I started trying right away.

"So, any news?" Bryan asked a few months into our marriage.

I knew what he referred to, and I shook my head.

My period arrived like clockwork every single month for the next three years.

I was crushed and devastated by my inability to get pregnant. I'd borne two children — my first child at 18 and the second at 20.

Now that I'm married and finally able to take care of children, I can't get pregnant?

Maybe it was the lack of children, or maybe he just didn't love me enough, but a year into our marriage, I discovered that Bryan had been unfaithful.

"How could you do this to me?" I screamed.

He was contrite. "I'm so sorry, Grace. Honey, please forgive me. I will do anything to make it up to you. Please."

"And she's pregnant?"

He nodded, shamefaced.

My rage faded into sadness, and a feeling of failure flooded me. *How was it that I couldn't get pregnant, but my husband's girlfriend did?*

Despite my heartbreak over my husband's unfaithfulness, we worked on our marriage.

But something was different, irrevocably so. The infidelity made sure of that.

I became desperate to leave the marriage.

Please, release me from this! I prayed to God often, hoping that he would give me the go-ahead to leave. I'm not sure what sign I expected, but it never came.

I spent two more years in this limbo, growing angrier with God each passing day.

My father thought it would be a good idea to get away, so we went to Israel for a week in August 2007. I completely relaxed on that trip with my father and a friend, and some of the tension from my unhappy marriage abated.

When I got back home, I learned that Bryan was in a relationship with two other women, who were also pregnant. I finally felt free to leave the marriage, and our divorce became final in February 2008.

I moved to Ridgefield, Washington, after my divorce so I could be close to my father. I also started attending my father's church, but I remained angry with God about the whole business with Bryan.

❧ ❧ ❧

A few months after I started attending my father's church, I still didn't feel like my life really had any purpose. Then our head pastor passed away. His death affected me deeply, and my struggles with depression intensified during that period.

Shortly after, I decided to focus on changing some things about my life, and I started with my physical health. I lost 75 of my 200 pounds, and when I was 38 years old, I joined the Army.

It ranked as the most powerful thing I'd ever done, and I felt extremely proud of myself.

Sadly, that feeling didn't last. I developed severe osteoarthritis in both knees and ended up being discharged from the Army nine short months after I joined.

That first month after my discharge from the Army, I traveled a lot. First, I went to Mississippi to visit my mother. We spent days shopping, in celebration of the 30 pounds I'd lost during Basic Training. Then, my father took me and my best friend to Italy for 10 days. The trip was a whirlwind of sightseeing trips and adventures, and I loved every minute of it.

The traveling gave me little time to dwell on the disappointment of having my Army dream cut short.

SEARCHING FOR PURPOSE

Afterward, I gradually settled into a normal routine, and a heavy, debilitating sadness set in. The days crept by in endless shades of gray, and as far as I knew, the sun never came up.

Those negative emotions filtered into everything. I shunned the company of others, hated going to work and found it nearly impossible to get out of bed on most days. On my days off from work, I lay in bed, listless, waiting for the relentless passing of time.

"Why is this happening to me?" I asked no one in particular as I drove home one day, tears pouring down my face.

Silence was the only answer.

ॐॐॐ

One thing gave me a glimmer of hope. Thinking about Dustin. We'd met in the Army and grew close within a short time. He possessed all the qualities I wanted in a man.

Maybe he was "the one." *Have I found what I've been looking for all these years?*

I called him a few days before Christmas to discuss our plans for me to visit.

"I'm so excited to see you, Dustin. I can barely wait," I gushed into the phone.

"Um, yeah, about that …"

His tone put me on my guard.

"I'm not sure it's such a good idea for you to visit."

I was stunned. What did he mean, "not a good idea"? And why was he just bringing it up?

"What? What are you saying, Dustin?"

"Look, Grace, I don't think we should see each other anymore. I'm not sure this relationship is going to work."

I felt my heart breaking — everything in my life seemed to be going sideways. Now this relationship, and all my hopes for it, slipped through my fingers.

What am I really living for? What is the point of my life?

I figured out the answer to both questions by the time I reached my home: nothing. I decided to end it all — to end the pain, the endless searching, the constant reaching for things that I could never have, things that I was never destined to have.

I thought about Aidan and the way he ended his pain.

While driving home, I busied myself wondering how to carry out my plan without alerting any of my four roommates. Our space was never empty, which would present a challenge.

There has to be a way. I'll find it.

To my surprise, when I entered, I found it empty.

Was this a sign? Was this the time to end it all?

I stood in the hallway, staring at the garage door, struggling with the idea of what to do with my precious dog. I couldn't leave her behind. I decided she'd be better off going with me.

As I stood there thinking about my next step, I felt something begin to change inside me. With sudden clarity, something dawned on me. It wasn't about daring God to rescue me; it was about wanting to be saved. God wasn't going to reach down and stop me. I'd reached rock bottom so that I would be left with nothing to reach for except God. I'd have to choose: end it all, continue looking for love in all the wrong places or turn fully to God.

I felt like I could hear him asking me, *Will you finally choose me, Grace?*

A force of emotion drove me to my knees. I sobbed uncontrollably as I knelt on the floor.

As the cleansing tears tracked twin rivers down my cheeks, I made my choice. I finally came full circle. I'd spent my life searching for something or someone to make me whole, battling deep unhappiness, mourning the loss of my two children. I thought about how my search for love through a series of sexual relationships ripped me away from God and put me on a self-destructive path.

I could choose to stop living in the past. I could move forward into a better future.

I thought about Aidan and how he ended his life, perhaps not realizing the pain it would inflict on those he left behind. In that moment on my knees, God showed me something very clearly: Suicide leaves a hole in the lives of those left behind, and we can either fill it with negative thoughts or with something positive.

I felt like God was offering me a second chance, and I grabbed it with both hands.

"I choose you!"

I made my choice, a choice to have a meaningful

relationship with God, to use my now-intimate understanding of suicide to help others.

I believed then that God allowed me to come so close to suicide so I would know what it felt like and could share my experience with others like me.

Gradually, the tears slowed, and my heart sang in joy. Finally, I had discovered the purpose for my life.

My angst turned to gratitude, and I looked away from that desolate door. Cheeks still wet, I found Hailey and clung to her. We weren't going to die that day.

ॐ ॐ ॐ

My life changed after what I think of as my hallway encounter with God. It's as though he flipped a switch and my constant desire to be in a relationship vanished.

I still battled with a deep sense of despondency, so I decided to change a few things about my life. In April 2012, I found another job, one which I enjoyed and looked forward to every day. That made it easier to handle getting up every day.

I also started attending church every Sunday, even though it sometimes felt like I was just going through the motions. Still, I knew I needed to stay close to God in order to maintain my rekindled relationship with him. I began to read my Bible every day, and that helped. I sought God and his strength for my situation, but I knew I also had a new role to play.

About six months after my near-escape from suicide, I visited a Christian counselor. Even though I knew I was moving in the right direction, it remained a slow and painful process, and I thought a counselor would be helpful.

It took a while to tell her my story, and when I finished, she said simply, "Grace, have you considered that you might be living with clinical depression?"

She asked the question in a casual manner, but I was floored. Relief flooded me. Even though it wasn't an official diagnosis by a psychologist, I thought it explained 90 percent of the problems I'd experienced throughout my life. And after everything I had gone through, I was finally in the right frame of mind to hear it.

"Clinical depression? You really think that's what I have?"

She nodded. "From all the things you've described, I would say it certainly sounds like it."

It did make sense. Until that point, I didn't understand how to make myself feel better, aside from trying to follow God, which was still something of a struggle. Having a diagnosis, even just a suggested one, gave me a place to start. I could research and manage a diagnosis. Finally, I had a name for the bleak hopelessness that had shadowed me all my life, and I learned to embrace my depression as an illness. I understood that it was something I would live with every day, and I was committed to doing everything I could to manage it.

Through it all, I rejoiced because I knew I was no longer alone. God was with me every step of the way, giving me the strength I needed for each day.

REFUGE

སོསོསོ

As my life changed, I learned to completely let go of what I wanted, what I always dreamed my life would be like, and accept that God had a bigger plan for me. Then, and only then, did I begin to experience true happiness, hidden in that acceptance and tangible pursuit of God's purpose.

I have never felt more at peace or more thankful for that peace. And it only grew out of the work I began to do for others.

I started to get this question whenever I spoke about mental illness: "Please, tell me I won't always feel this way."

I never had to think about my answer. "No, you won't. Things will get better, I promise."

I became able to reassure them because of my personal experience. "I've been there, in that dark pit of despair that feels completely overwhelming. But, today, I live with absolute happiness and joy. And one day, so will you."

My purpose in life has become preventing suicides, and specifically, lowering the rate of suicide in the Army. It feels amazing to know that my life has a point.

It became so clear to me, it may as well be written in black and white: I believe that God shapes our life experiences to give us each a passion and a purpose for a specific cause or issue. That way, everyone is working on something different, and all the causes and issues are covered.

SEARCHING FOR PURPOSE

I've learned that my work to help others is extremely important. As I pursued my work in suicide prevention, I became content that I am exactly where God wants me to be.

This is what I was born to do.

All those years, I thought I was waiting on God, only to find out that, all along, he was waiting for me.

PICTURE PERFECT
The Story of Jessica and Caleb
Written by Emily Miller

The doors of the clinic shut quickly, as if waving us on. I walked slowly next to Caleb until we reached our black Nissan. Clutching the handle, I ducked into the passenger side and mechanically clicked my seatbelt into its blurred red target.

Caleb pulled out, wheels hurling fragments of scattered rocks beneath. With nothing left to say, the half-hour trip home stretched long before us.

Not wanting to delay the news any longer, my fingers punched the familiar numbers of home. The phone rang in the distance as I inhaled deeply. My sister answered.

"Hello?" Her voice flowed soft and steady, tinted with hopeful expectation — her hope enough to sting.

Fresh tears silently ran down my flushed cheeks. I swallowed hard. My throat burned.

"Jess?" She invited me to continue.

I exploded in sobs.

"Oh, Jessica."

ॐॐॐ

REFUGE

Jessica

Growing up, my childhood bordered on perfection. I spent many hours playing with my two siblings in Woodland, Washington, a town known for its forested ambience. We lived in a log cabin and loved hiking through trails on weekend camping trips. Memories of childhood are comforting, like the nostalgia one feels when watching reruns of *Little House on the Prairie.*

My mother worked as a nurse but always put her family first. She demonstrated this priority in a million little ways. Mom always made breakfast, usually eggs or pancakes, gave us sheets to tie up as hammocks and if we were ever scared during the night, she would guide us back to our room and stay there until we fell asleep.

She also knew how to make an occasion special. On snow days, she baked cinnamon rolls and poured us steaming hot chocolate made with real milk. She, as well as my dad, loved us kids, and we knew it.

Yes, I had a "picture-perfect" childhood, it seemed.

The summer before the seventh grade, I started working for my dad on the golf course. I dutifully helped maintain the grounds along with my sister, Erin, and brother, David. The golf course superintendent, the "greens keeper," our dad, displayed a work ethic most commonly pinned on American-bred farmers. Yet, his hard work didn't callous him. He was gentle, the kind of dad who takes his girls to breakfast even after they're married.

PICTURE PERFECT

৵৵৵

I first met Caleb in youth group. He was in college, and he volunteered his time and went on many trips with us. By the time I enrolled in George Fox University as a sophomore, Caleb had already graduated with an electrical engineering degree and taken a job with Intel. Although I was an hour away in Oregon, we remained in contact through similar social groups and eventually decided to date.

We dated my sophomore and half of my junior year. I got to know Caleb through the phone calls and emails we exchanged during the week. He was kind, caring, full of integrity, intelligent and a gentleman. I never questioned his feelings for me and loved him in return. Plus, he was a ton of fun! Normal weekend activities included: playing games, hiking, rafting, camping with our families, going to the beach, skiing, attending concerts and occasionally watching plays. I knew Caleb would make a great husband and, someday, a great father.

The following summer, I lived at home and worked at the golf course. While at work one day, Dad told me to take the next day off. I thought this odd. Apparently Mom needed some help at the house. I didn't care. It provided a good excuse to sleep in.

The door creaked slightly, and in walked Mom. I pulled myself up, rubbing the sleep from my eyes as she turned on the light.

"Caleb?" He smiled at me from the doorway. "What are you doing here? You're supposed to be working."

"I took the day off." He thrust forth the vibrant bouquet of pink daisies and red roses close to my face so I could smell their sweet aroma.

I inhaled deeply, baby's breath tickling my nose. "Thanks, babe."

"I have a special day prepared starting with breakfast, so come to the kitchen when you're ready."

Mom took the flowers from me, and Caleb stole one last glance before closing the door behind him. I leapt toward my closet and shuffled through the hangers, finally choosing a brown spaghetti-strapped dress based on my instincts and his tie. As I stood in front of the mirror picking out eye shadow, the piano's soft melody floated into my room, as did the smell of eggs and sausage. I could only assume Mom was cooking. I applied mascara and blush before smearing gloss on lips that wouldn't stop smiling.

❧❧❧

Caleb

Jessica sauntered into the kitchen from her bedroom just off the main floor. My eyes met hers. Her face glowed with anticipation as she walked toward the table and sat down. Sun beamed in through the dining room window, hinting at the day's forecast. Jessica and I casually picked through our eggs, plopping spoonfuls of fruit onto our plates.

After cleaning up, we played a game of Cribbage to kill time.

"Well, should we get going?" I asked.

"Sure. Let's go! Where are we going?" Her eyes pried for more information.

"I guess you'll have to figure that out. But first, you might want to go put on something a little more comfortable."

I drove Jessica 40 minutes north to a small airport. We quickly located the private pilot who proudly showed us his plane. Jessica eagerly climbed in the cabin first and started situating her seatbelt. The pilot pulled me aside.

"I'm sorry, son, but the turn of weather has necessitated a change of plans," he whispered. "It's impossible to land in Vancouver. I'm not even sure if we'll make it to St. Helens."

I swallowed my disappointment and climbed in the back next to Jessica.

Our plane followed the Columbia River up to Astoria. The propeller spun loudly, limiting opportunities for conversation. Jessica and I gazed out either side of the plane, commenting now and then on the scenery below. As the pilot looped back toward Kelso, his voice broke into our headsets.

"The weather's subsided a bit. I'm going to try to make it to Mount St. Helens via the Toutle River."

Jessica and I exchanged eager smiles. I wondered if she saw a future together like I did. Together, we gazed through the slight haze, pointing at the quaint towns nestled below. As we closed in on the mountain, the clouds opened up to blue sky, and there it was right before us. We were able to fly right next to the mountain, with its entire north side missing, allowing us to peer into the crater. The careening black remnants of lava still remained cemented down the side, as if they were walking trails.

Back in the car, we drove south to Vancouver to switch to the blue-green 1963 Buick Special convertible that my dad had waiting for us. Fixing up old cars was a hobby of Dad's. Over the years, he had collected five classic cars with the hope of giving one to each of his four boys when he retired.

The weather cleared, allowing for the top to go down as Jessica and I headed east up the Columbia River Gorge. Tree-enameled cliffs lined our route until we reached Cascade Locks, where a sternwheeler was docked and loading. We joined a number of cruisers lining the dock and soon made our way to the top deck where we could watch the huge paddle wheel re-circulating water to propel us farther into the historic scenery.

As the afternoon started to fade, we drove over the Bridge of the Gods, whose underbelly stretched wide across the river's expanse. As we drove back to Washington, looking at the wide-open sky, all our dreams seemed possible. Wind blazed through our hair, and conversation quieted only in lulls of admiration.

☙☙☙

Jessica

We wound our way down Highway 14 and finally pulled into a small lot. Caleb unloaded the stowaway backpack and lobbed its weight over his shoulders. At the base of the trailhead, he took my hand, and we started making our ascent. I knew that day was special, but I didn't feel anxious — just happy. The full day of activities meant a lot. The hike itself felt especially meaningful since, throughout our relationship, we had hiked on nearly every trail within a large radius.

The day — the details — it was all perfect.

౿౿౿

Caleb

We stopped four miles up the mountain, staking our claim to a ridge that overlooked the gorge. I pulled out a blanket from the backpack, flapping its sides against the breeze. I smoothed it over golden grass, and Jessica sat down. She didn't need an invitation.

The sky paled, and clouds faded into violet shadows. Beneath the sunset's orange glow, I told Jessica how much she meant to me and serenaded her with a song I had written just days before. We locked eyes, and I took her slender hand in mine, slipping on her finger a promise I was committed to keep.

౿౿౿

Jessica

In 2005, nearly two years after getting married, I finished nursing school and took a job at a nearby hospital as a float pool nurse. Throughout school, I never felt confident this was what I wanted to do for the rest of my life, and the job itself stressed me to my hair's roots. Every night I came in to my 12-hour shift blind — I showed up, and my supervisor would assign me a new floor. So, I didn't develop relationships with my co-workers, and I had no assignment to call "home."

I was miserable.

At night, I would wake up panicked that I had forgotten to record a vital sign or a hundred other little things. My stomach sickened thinking about all I might have done wrong or forgotten to do. I felt I could never do enough. I was the only person in the world who believed it, for every time I placed a phone call to retrace my steps, all had been taken care of. Perfectionism turned out to be a fraudulent skill, an enemy, and stress my companion.

It was during this time, Caleb and I decided to get pregnant.

I moved to the birth center, working as a postpartum nurse, in the summer of 2006. My situation changed, but my barrenness didn't, compounding the stress and inadequacy I felt. I didn't understand how my sister and so many others could get pregnant so effortlessly. Caleb and I tried a little longer before we finally investigated fertility options. We also purchased land at this time, dreaming of the children who would make our house a home.

❧❧❧

"Jessica. Caleb." Dr. Johnson firmly shook each of our hands. I forced a distracted smile, bracing myself for the unknown.

Dr. Johnson took a seat. "Good news. Your results show no abnormalities, which means you have a special case we like to call 'unexplained infertility.' I really don't see any reason why you can't have a successful pregnancy." He paused, his brown eyes dancing with optimism.

"Well, that's great! Thank you very much."

"Yes, thank you," I broke in. "So, what's the next step?"

❧❧❧❧

A few months later, Caleb and I sat in the office of the reproductive medicine clinic we were consulting. The suggested fertility treatment ended successfully, just as Dr. Johnson predicted. Once we had a little push, getting pregnant was a breeze. Caleb and I beamed with excitement. We looked forward to the tiny hands that would soon appear on the ultrasound, the contemplating of names and the clothes that would line the baby's closet. It was hard not to stumble as our feet ran ahead. We told ourselves over and over again we just had to make it through the next appointment.

After waiting for some time in the sterilized, blandly decorated room, the lab technician came in to check my Human Chorionic Gonadotropin (hCG) levels. Another technician rechecked them two days later to see if the hormone levels were rising appropriately. Then Caleb and I drove home again to wait for the results.

"I'm sorry, Jessica, but it looks like your hCG levels aren't rising as they should be ..." The nurse's voice rang with compassion, but I wanted her to stop. I didn't want to hear the cold singular pop of hope. She continued hesitantly. "I suspect you will probably miscarry in a few days." She paused, waiting.

I mumbled a response.

"Again, Jessica, I'm really sorry. If you're willing to proceed, I can make you another appointment?" Again, she waited.

"Yes, sure, that would be fine."

๛๛๛

Five months later, I was pregnant again. At week eight, my belly swelled, no matter how slightly, giving us confidence. The nurse squeezed gel onto the probe and provided us proof of the baby inside. The monitor picked it up! His or her heart rhythmically beat strong — with regularity — a sign that a healthy life grew inside of me.

Dr. Patterson, my OB doctor, spoke in congratulatory tones, but cautioned us on the way out. We familiarized ourselves with the risks. Even so, my heart ballooned with excitement. Caleb and I made lighthearted conversation all the way home.

Two weeks later, we returned for another checkup.

PICTURE PERFECT

The probe dug deep into my belly. The doctor approached the baby from various angles, but there was nothing. We'd lost the heartbeat. Dressed and upright, I heard another rendition suggesting further efforts. My mind went numb realizing this wasn't an easy fix and was perhaps something that never would be fixed.

Back at work, I continued taking vitals of countless successful women and their babies. Most days, I blocked out all emotional attachments, but not all days. *God, we have such a good home — a good life — to offer. How can you not let us have a baby?* I tried to separate myself, but some days the ugly truth left me ashamed. I was jealous.

And it wasn't even these women who made me the most upset. Having wished all along that my sister, Erin, and I could raise our children together, I felt left behind. It was an awkward joy — her having two kids and me having none. I wanted to embrace her happiness, but instead a dark sadness settled deep inside the pit of my chest. I loved my nephews but longed for children of my own.

That longing and the support of others — especially my sister who, through it all, proved her love to me again and again — enabled me to persevere. Caleb and I met Dr. Johnson again to see what more we could do. At the end of our consultation, he proposed in vitro fertilization. We proceeded with the treatment.

Nearly a year later, in July of 2009, we conceived for the third time, three years after our first try. I was overjoyed but not relieved. Not wanting to let my heart get attached too soon, I cautiously endured the same preliminary tests and smiled through the same appointments. Again, Caleb and I heard the baby's heartbeat at eight weeks. And again, two weeks later, it — the baby — was gone.

After hanging up with Erin, I fell silent as Caleb drove us along I-5 toward home. Caleb followed me into the house carefully searching for any clues as to how to respond or comfort, but he received none. I wanted to be alone. I entered our bedroom, without flipping on the light. I sank down to the carpet and leaned against the footboard. All hope was gone. Finally safe from prying eyes, I broke, unashamed. My head exploded with loud sobs as my stomach contorted fiendishly. No clear thought came, only pain — a distorted congealing of loneliness, helplessness, defeat and blame. *I had failed at carrying a baby.* Fresh waves of sorrow washed over my sick stomach.

In that honest moment, something changed. I felt wrapped in love, comforted. I do believe, at that moment, Jesus took me in his arms. I welcomed his embrace and the peace of his presence that commanded every distorted emotion to leave. Warmth lubricated my aching heart, and I rested like a child does when consoled and loved after experiencing the pain of an unfair world.

"Blessed are those who mourn, for they will be comforted." I repeated the verse from Matthew, chapter 5, again. *Blessed are those who mourn.* Jesus' most famous sermon, one I'd heard numerous times growing up, now had meaning. *Blessed.* I said the word again and again, desperately delving for the treasure inside. Through the deep pain, I felt blessed to be comforted by God.

I lingered longer and leaned into the presence that held me there. *It's okay to be sad.* I stared into the dark, shadowed lines of my bedroom furniture. In that profound darkness, I knew everything would be okay. I sensed Jesus listening to me, answering me and, above all, comforting me.

꙳꙳꙳

Breaking news ricocheted from screen to screen in the United States as Haitians shook in the aftermath of an earthquake topping seven on the Richter scale. The wrecking ball that hit just west of Port-au-Prince cost thousands their lives and left many more homeless. Humanitarian aid rushed in to prop up tents as mothers propped up children. As close friends of ours from Ridgefield Church of the Nazarene made their way to help in the aftermath, I decided to go along. My mother, also a nurse, came, too. After arriving, we traveled north to Children of the Promise (COTP), an organization that exists to provide for the needs of babies and infants who've been orphaned or abandoned.

While in Haiti, Mom and I dispensed medicine and vitamins and helped where we could by providing medical care, but we primarily played with the recovering children. It was at the Infant Care Center that I met Ricky and fell in love. I went without a hint of expectation, but throughout the trip, my heart flickered with the new possibility of adoption.

Still tired from the flight home, I recounted as much of the two weeks to Caleb as I could remember. He listened hard as I described the far-reaching devastation. It made him feel good that our friends Lindsey and Chris were planning to stay in Haiti long term. I continued on, naming children and telling their stories. I slowed when portraying Ricky, hoping Caleb would feel the same connection I did.

"I'm sorry, Jessica. I just don't know if I'm ready to start looking at adoption."

I felt disappointed but not defeated. Adoption was something we hadn't previously considered. So, I continued investigating the possibility of adoption and talking to Caleb about it. He eventually warmed up to the idea. That summer, we started pursuing Ricky.

We worked hard on the cumbersome paperwork our agent had sent, but it wasn't long before we received a phone call that Ricky was no longer up for adoption. An agent had already matched him with another family. I was devastated at the outcome of yet *another* closed door. Hanging up the phone felt like closing a book and tossing it aside without ever knowing if I'd open it — or even pick it up — again.

I wanted a baby and was open to adoption when I knew the baby. Now that I couldn't have Ricky, whose personality and story I knew, I didn't know if I wanted a baby at all. I reflected back on my picture-perfect childhood. I always imagined my children would grow up the same way. I couldn't imagine raising a child whose questions were too big for my admittedly sheltered upbringing. What would I say to a child who felt abandoned and broken when all I had ever known was acceptance? My heart grew heavy thinking this could be the end of our journey.

I tried to focus on the house we'd started building. We remained busy with construction and legalities since we were the general contractors. Still, the house didn't distract me from my innermost desire. At night, I dreamt of a dark-skinned little boy whose image captivated my heart throughout the day. I couldn't shake the desire to have children and believed a baby was within reach. Caleb agreed we could continue pursuing adoption with COTP, but we remained busy, only getting five hours of sleep each night.

The added responsibilities, in addition to work, made the winter months waltz by almost unnoticed until tulips trumpeted the arrival of a new season.

❧❧❧

Caleb

Our adoption coordinator sent us profiles of three little boys she thought would be good candidates. Sitting down, exhausted, Jessica and I slowly read through each one. It was in this moment that a light flipped on. Seeing a face was my point of connection in the "birthing" process, much like it is in the biological realm when a mother carries a baby for nine months and the father supports on standby trying to understand the mother's intrinsic attraction.

Both Jessica and I felt drawn to one child in particular, Wilnes. His profile eased the fears we shared of having a child we couldn't provide for emotionally. Instead of difficulties, we read of a "very sweet little boy who smiles a lot, loves to share with his friends, loves to play with balls and also loves music."

I turned his picture over in my head again and again trying to grasp the reality of finally being a father. I couldn't wait to meet the little boy in the blue baseball shirt.

༖༖༖

Jessica

I snaked my way through the maze that would become our dining room. The walls were skeletal bones without sheetrock and the floors merely plywood. A makeshift table, again plywood, supported an assortment of tools for my (or Caleb's) choosing pleasure. I busied myself, working on some odds and ends while Caleb worked his regular job.

The phone rang. *Is this it?*

"Hello?" I stood near the window looking out over the Lewis River Valley to the hills beyond.

"Hi, Jessica. This is Julia calling about Wilnes. How are you?"

"Fine, thanks."

"Listen, I'm calling to inform you that you have officially been matched with Wilnes. He's yours."

Tears welled up. The prior few years of painstaking prayer and effort culminated in that one moment — the afternoon of March 18, 2011 — the day God answered our prayers. I finished the conversation with a burning knot swelling in my throat, asking Julia, our adoption coordinator, several times if it was official.

"Yes, you are free to tell the world that a beautiful 2-year-old boy named Wilnes will be your son."

The tree line blurred, and I mouthed unintelligible praise and thanks to God. I wanted to dance and scream, but I was suddenly hushed by immobilizing awe. I stood in a house unfinished, a story unfinished and a life unfinished. It wasn't my idea of perfection, but it was perfect. I pictured Wilnes making our house a home.

Caleb was equally thrilled to hear the news. That afternoon, Julia sent more pictures. I beamed with excitement but decided to wait for Caleb so we could view them together. When he got home, we immediately booted up the computer and logged onto our email. We studied each picture meticulously, then ordered prints on Costco's Web site.

The next evening, I sat at my parents' table. The whole family, minus my brother and his wife who couldn't make it, gathered to celebrate the March birthdays. Between mouthfuls, I wholeheartedly attempted to join in the animated conversation, but I was distracted.

Finally, unable to wait any longer, I abruptly lunged from my seat, scooped up Erin's gift and shoved it into her hands.

Mom continued eating.

Erin carefully tore the paper and looked at me wild-eyed. "Is this him? Is this him?"

Everyone turned to look at us.

Crying, Erin turned the picture around so everyone could see. I stood next to her brimming with pleasure, waiting for the news to register.

Not knowing what to make of the scene, my nearly 4-year-old nephew grabbed the picture. "Aw, he's a cute little guy, isn't he?"

Everyone howled with laughter, wiping away the tears that just kept coming.

ॐॐॐ

Early that fall, we put the finishing touches on our house and began getting ready to move in. We were also due to get on a plane in a few days to fill out more paperwork and see Wilnes, but something was wrong. I felt increasingly strange and grew disturbed when I kept making frequent trips to the restroom when on any other day I had an unusual propensity to hold my bladder. I knew I didn't have an infection, so I sheepishly drove to the dollar store.

Laughing, crying and praising God, I scrutinized the one dark pink stripe that showed up and the slight one that followed. *WHAT? You've got to be kidding.* I couldn't deny the results, nor could I trust a test I paid a dollar for, so I went to Walmart to get a digital foolproof test. This time, the screen read clear.

P-R-E-G-N-A-N-T.

That night Caleb and I fell into bed, exhausted. The room was dim, and I pulled out the pregnancy test, handing it to Caleb.

"What's this?" he mumbled, examining its shape. He had no idea, so I jumped out of bed to turn on a brighter light.

"What? Really?"

My skin pricked with goose bumps as I stared at Caleb, nodding. We hadn't seen the fertility doctor since before my last miscarriage and were so busy with the house and the adoption, we never even thought *this* could happen. We were pregnant! We kissed and cried, too excited to sleep.

Eventually, our glee wore down to a sober conversation.

I didn't want to get my hopes up, but something felt different this time. I sensed Jesus answering our prayers. Maybe not in the way we initially expected but answering them nonetheless.

Adding to the excitement was the timing. My sister was pregnant with her third child.

❧❧❧

REFUGE

Caleb

I climbed up the metal staircase that stretched to the balcony. Jessica followed behind me.

We breathed in the hot, muggy Haitian air our son was accustomed to. Lindsey invited us to sit down on some lawn chairs. Lindsey and Chris worked for Children of the Promise and had hosted Wilnes in their home for four months prior to our arrival in order to acclimate him to a family setting.

Lindsey returned juggling a couple bottles of water. "Sorry, guys. Wilnes is still taking his nap. If he doesn't wake up soon, I'll get him."

We could hardly wait to see our little boy.

After a while, Wilnes quietly toddled out behind Lindsey. He stood at a distance and stared apprehensively. We stared back commenting on how cute he looked and how nice it was to finally meet him. Suddenly, Jessica initiated a game of peek-a-boo. Wilnes smiled.

We spent the rest of the day with Lindsey and Kenny, her adopted son. Lindsey gave us a tour of the compound, while Jessica and I pushed the boys around in strollers. Instinctively, I wanted to favor Wilnes — he was my son. However, I knew protocol told me otherwise. This was a preliminary visit, meaning the relationship needed to remain neutral for the protection of children whose adoptive parents fell through.

However, I did get to take him in my arms and throw him toward the clouds — something I did with my nephews and always imagined I would do with my son.

PICTURE PERFECT

This game of throwing my son to the sky felt like the realization of a dream come true.

❧❧❧

Jessica

In the months following, we moved into our new house and prepared for the arrival of our boys.

Caleb and I remained hesitant during the first few months of pregnancy and while going through all the same appointments we had experienced prior to our miscarriages. I dreamed of the baby who would smile at me and call me mommy, believing this would be the one.

Still, a few hiccups kept me grounded. At each appointment, I braced myself for bad news but heard none. After nearly six months, I finally believed this was how Jesus truly wanted to answer our prayers, and I allowed myself to accept the gift and take pictures of my protruding belly. This time, I was going to know my baby's personality.

In April, Mom, my close friend Grace and sister-in-law Katy hosted a baby shower at church, Ridgefield Nazarene. The large room filled quickly with nearly 40 people all crammed into a circle laughing and talking, as women do. Blue decorations punctuated the otherwise bland room creating a celebratory atmosphere complete with cake, games and gifts. Halfway through the shower, I began opening my gifts. Grace handed me the next bag. It was from a woman named Polly. Surprised, I took the folded blanket and held it up. The room of women oohed and aahed. I looked at Polly.

Polly was the sister of my friend Joan who had recently passed away. I loved both sisters, but I was especially close to Joan. She always embraced me with a warm hug on Sunday mornings. Joan embodied faithfulness and was encouraging to see on a regular basis. Her worn face spoke of wisdom, and her knobby knuckles spoke of work. For years, the sisters labored together sewing blankets. Ever since I could remember, every baby born into our church family received a blanket from Polly and Joan. After Joan died, Polly stopped making blankets.

"Polly, it's beautiful. Thank you!" I smiled genuinely, knowing it was handmade.

"Well, now. There's a story to that blanket." She faced the other women, her voice shaky. "Most of you know my sister. Well, since she died, I stopped sewing and quilting. I gave everything away — just couldn't do it without her. But, Jessica, when I found out about our long-awaited miracle baby, I really, really wanted to give you something special from me and Joan — something handmade. I had one last boy blanket and wanted to give it to you, but it had already been spoken for by my relative. Since I only had one, I thought I better give it to her, even though she's having a girl." Polly smiled wryly. "As it turns out, just days before your shower, I found a girl blanket tucked in a back closet that I gave to my relative instead."

I ran my hand over the white blanket's careful stitching and appliqué pattern of small boys dressed in overalls and tilted caps. I was sad Joan wasn't alive to see the answer to her prayers, but I knew her love would forever be tenderly wrapped around my two boys.

"Thank you, Polly. This means a lot."

సౌసౌసౌ

Caleb

Jessica called me from work to alert me she was having contractions. She'd started having occasional contractions halfway through the pregnancy, so we were used to what they were, but this time they didn't go away. She was in labor. We checked in with the midwife, walked around the nearby neighborhood and went back to find that Jessica was further dilated. Shortly into laboring, I knew it was going to be a long night. Thankfully, her sister and mom were there to help.

After a few hours that stretched endlessly, the midwife gave Jessica the go-ahead to push. A few minutes later, a nurse got close to my wife's face warning her that this might be the most important moment of her life. She continued to push, but she seemed dazed. The baby's heart rate was dropping. A doctor came in with a vacuum, and then, without warning, a swarm of doctors and nurses entered ready to assist if need be. I felt helpless. *God, this could go either way. Save our baby!* The room remained tense, and all I could do was pray and silently reciprocate the worried reflections surrounding me. Suddenly, a piercing cry cut through thick intensity. The medical team surrounding us, some of whom were Jessica's co-workers, stood grounded in that one moment — eyes glistening. Jacob was born on May 22, 2012. Seconds later, the doctor placed him in Jessica's arms.

His face captured my attention, as I knew his was the face of answered prayer.

Five weeks later, I boarded a plane for the homecoming of our other son. Upon arriving in Cap-Haitien, volunteers from COTP picked me up in a maroon Toyota outfitted with a snorkel. We weren't planning on scuba diving, but apparently it makes for good airflow in a country where dust and rising water levels can hamper a vehicle's performance. I sat on top of supply boxes in the back.

After running errands for the upcoming Fourth of July party, we jostled our way up to the COTP compound where Lindsey was waiting at the guesthouse. Chris would be out of town until midway through the week. As during our prior visit, Wilnes was napping. I went to the first-floor room located near the volunteer kitchen to drop off my luggage, which wasn't much considering most of it had gotten lost by the airline.

I sat talking on the balcony when Lindsey brought him out. Wilnes walked right up to me and pointed his chubby finger. "Papa." Lindsey coached him to say "Daddy," just as they had practiced. He climbed up on my lap, and I squeezed him tight multiple times, reassuring myself he was forever mine. Lindsey left the room and returned with the picture book Jessica and I had sent. Together they went through all the rigmarole of who's who in his new family.

"Who's that?"

"Mommy." His voice quiet but sure.

"And who's this?" Lindsey turned, pointing to me.

"Daddy!"

After our reintroduction, we went on a walk, played at the playground and glided along the zip line. Everywhere we went, Wilnes made sure to grab my hand. I threw him up in the air and gave him "zerberts" on his stomach, igniting a fitful bout of giggles. Then we went back home. On our way we passed by rabbits and looked at the ongoing construction. There remained one building that still didn't have a roof on, but it was coming along.

Lindsey set plates of steaming pasta down, then sat Wilnes next to me. He climbed onto his knees making himself tall enough for the big table. When we finished eating, Wilnes promptly took our plates to the sink. Afterward, he sat by me for story time. We also played with some trains until it was bath time. His lips puckered in frustration when he thought I wasn't coming. He grabbed my hand, pulling me toward the bathroom. Regardless of what our little boy understood, most probably with mixed emotions, it seemed he knew we had a special relationship.

Slow transition marked the remainder of the week. Lindsey switched Wilnes completely over to my care to create normalcy and routine. He attached himself to me quickly and grew uneasy of any changes, such as going back to Lindsey and Chris' house to get his haircut. I carried him up the stairs and managed to cut his hair myself. Back in the guesthouse, I introduced him to various toys. He played with his plane, coloring pad or blue Nalgene water bottle before gingerly putting each one back in his new zebra backpack. When outside, he liked taking walks, pushing dump trucks or announcing any airplane overhead, which happened to be quite often since COTP sits below the Cap-Haitien flight path.

The day always ended with a bedtime routine: cleaning up, putting on his jammies, reading four books to him, singing two songs — the "Alphabet Song" and "Amazing Grace" — and saying a prayer.

కీకీకీ

The morning of July 7, I woke up at 4:45 to do some last-minute packing. After breakfast, a handful of the COTP crew greeted us outside the guesthouse in the pale morning to say goodbye. Wilnes spent a few minutes with each person, then climbed into the truck, waving goodbye.

Chris suggested I count the number of times Wilnes shouted "airplane." *One, two, three* ... I stopped counting after 33, thinking it would make for a long trip.

"Hey, Chris, you have the tickets, right?"

"Yeah, right here." He handed them to me.

"I don't see my ticket." I rummaged through my backpack as the ticket agent stared.

"Oh, man, I must have left it with my luggage stubs."

The ticket agent stared at me a second longer. "You can buy another one for $120."

I hastily pulled out the cash. My son stood next to me patiently watching the whole scene. The woman punched some keys on the slightly antiquated keyboard before handing me another ticket. Chris waved, staying behind to make sure the luggage made it on our flight.

I gave Wilnes one of the snacks Jessica had packed so his ears wouldn't pop. He happily munched during takeoff and landing. Next, to our surprise, a taxi driver in an air-conditioned Isuzu Trooper took us to the second airport. After checking in and passing security, we waited at the gate, and Wilnes dug in his backpack for a few cars and plastic animals. After a while, a woman handed me a yellow balloon, which my boy and I batted back and forth. I watched the excitement dance in his eyes, and my heart melted at the thought that this was only the beginning of many happy years together.

దిందింది

Jessica

We arrived early at PDX, the Portland International Airport, anticipating Caleb and Wilnes' arrival. Soon the waiting area filled. A crowd of nearly 50 people surrounded me — friends, family and church members. I bounced Jacob in my arms while anticipating the moment I had imagined for days — no, years.

I spotted Wilnes first. He walked confidently, keeping up with Caleb's long strides. The crowd broke out in an immutable roar. The sound echoed distantly as tears immediately pierced my eyes, blurring my vision. I quickly wiped them away, studying my boy's orange shirt, zebra backpack, gait and straight-laced face. Tears streamed down Caleb's face as he embraced me. He took Jacob, and I bent down to lift my little boy, cradling him close.

We drove home that day in awe and probably exhaustion. I kept looking back, marveling at God's provision and timing and the faces of my two boys. Jacob stared, wide-eyed, and Wilnes looked out the window, taking in his new surroundings. I wondered what questions he might ask or how his needs would change. I didn't know what the future held, but I no longer worried. We pulled into the garage and walked in the house.

"Shoes off! Shoes off, Daddy." My observant son sat down, flicking off his Crocs. He then timidly toddled off to explore, stopping at the built-in swing hanging from the ceiling in our living room. I held Jacob, bathing in the laughter that filled our home.

Watching our two happy boys overshadowed all those dark days — the day I called Erin, the day I sat alone in my bedroom, the day we heard another apology — all those days of unanswered prayers.

The whole time I'd felt blinded by circumstances, but later I saw evidence of Jesus continually working to develop a picture that would one day be perfection, in his presence forever. It is slow and sometimes painful, but some things simply can't be rushed. Life takes time to process, to create, to develop. I wanted to freeze the moment, me holding Jacob and Daddy gently pushing Wilnes in the swing.

I did capture it and have captured our family a million more times through the lens of a camera. God kept developing the bigger picture, slipping in more surprises.

We got pregnant again.

THE CHOICE OF JOY
The Story of Sarah

Written by Lisa Bradshaw

"I love you, Mom." I stroked the small of her trembling back. "It will be okay."

I closed my eyes tightly as his open hand came toward my mom's face again. When I heard the slap and felt my mom fall to the floor, I opened my eyes again, trying not to cry.

"It's okay, Mom," I whispered.

This time, my mom stayed down. She did not try to get up.

"It's okay, Mom." I started to cry. "Just stay down."

With one swift kick to my mom's left arm, my dad wiped his forehead and left the room. He had worked up a sweat.

I helped my mom up from the floor and led her upstairs to her bedroom. She was crying and had a pounding headache, so when my dad finally passed out on the couch downstairs, my mom sent my oldest sister, Amy, to sneak by him and get her a few aspirin tablets from the kitchen.

None of this was new to us, especially to my mom.

❧❧❧

REFUGE

I was 5 years old when I stopped hiding in my bedroom while my dad beat my mom. He was not interested in hurting me, except for the pain he caused me to see him hurt her. My older brother and sister got the worst of it — I was just a spectator.

My dad was not just a mean drunk, he was a drunk who was mean. Whether he was drunk or sober, all of us feared him and only breathed easy when he got hauled off to jail for a few days or when my mom kicked him out overnight, even if he just passed out in his truck parked outside our house.

I had four sisters and two brothers, and each of us suffered in our own way. Fear was a constant in our house, perhaps because there were so many of us to hurt and so many who wanted to hurt us. My earliest memories as a child are of watching my brother getting beat up by my dad and my sisters and me receiving money from my uncles and cousins for sitting on their laps and touching them on their private areas. I did not know what any of it meant, I just knew it did not feel right, and it made me fearful and uncomfortable.

As terrible as he was — beating my brother and sister or spewing cruel words without provocation — Dad was not who I most feared.

It was his brothers. And their sons. The men who made my sisters and me do things we did not want to do. Over and over again.

I was 5 years old the first time one of my older cousins took me into a bedroom and molested me. The pain was excruciating. He eventually stopped and left me in the bed crying.

When I was 6, Mom left me with my father's father, my grandfather, for an hour while she went to the grocery store. It was the first time I'd ever been alone with him, and he wasted no time pinning me down, even though I did not stop crying. He did not care.

When my mom got home, I was still crying and told her what my grandpa had done.

"You sick, dirty old man! You stay away from my girl!" she screamed at him, enraged and crying.

He left laughing smugly, knowing he could be back anytime he wanted, and there was nothing my mom could do to stop him. Not even my own father tried to stop him.

My sisters and I each suffered in the dreaded bedroom with the men from my father's family, my older sister and brother got beatings while being told they were no good and my mom did her best to keep herself and the rest of us alive.

My dad did not work, unless it was long enough to get money together for a bottle of booze. He earned nothing toward providing us food or shelter. We moved from place to place, often leaving in the middle of the night to avoid paying the past-due rent. My parents had no money to pay it, anyway.

We lived on welfare and often stayed with my dad's family, presenting his dad, brothers and nephews additional access to us girls. My own father tried to molest my oldest sister, Amy, but she cried and that made him angry, so he kicked her out of the bedroom and hardly spoke to her again. He treated her more cruelly than the rest of his daughters. She lived a tortured existence. Dad made sure of it.

"Stand there! If you don't move, you won't get hurt!" Dad yelled at Amy while he forced my brothers to throw darts at her. She was too young to know that he had put tape on the ends of the darts to prevent her from serious bodily harm, but the mental abuse was enough.

"Please stop! Please stop, Daddy!" she cried, but that just made it more fun for him as he and my brothers taunted her and kept throwing darts.

My dad never put his hands on me, but I still feared being left alone with him because I saw what he did to my mother, sisters and brothers. All I knew to do was stick close to my mom, and I did.

During a trip to California with two of my older sisters, my dad and my grandpa, I ended up alone with my grandpa the first night there. Over and over again, he told me to get in bed with him.

"Come on, come to bed with me, Sarah," he tried to persuade me.

"No, I'm sleeping on the floor."

"Just for a little while," he tried to coerce me.

"No!"

Every time he asked, I refused, and for whatever reason, he did not force me to get in bed with him.

I'd begged my mom to let me go on the trip, but as I lay there, I cried out for her.

THE CHOICE OF JOY

"Mom, I want to come home," I whispered, in tears. "Why did you let me come here?"

Maybe she figured I would be safe with my sisters, but none of us was safe. That was the first time I questioned why my mom had not protected me.

When I got home, I ran into my mom's arms.

"I missed you so much, Mom! I was afraid I would never see you again!"

"You are fine. You're home now," she said, so matter-of-fact, as she hugged me, then walked with me into the house.

Even though my grandpa had had his way with me many other times before that night in California, he never did again. I do not know if he lost interest in me as I got older or if he just lost all desire in general, but I was free of him after that, and I feared him less and less.

Curiously, it was a tragic accident — not caused by my dad or any of the men who regularly or relentlessly caused our suffering — that prompted my mom to fight back.

It was duck hunting season. My brothers and uncle were out hunting one Sunday morning. They were standing in a field when my oldest brother, Steve, was fidgeting with the safety on his shotgun, and the gun fired by accident.

He blew a hole right through my brother Jeremy's back.

Blood splattered everywhere, Jeremy fell to the ground barely breathing and Steve screamed uncontrollably, nearly going into shock over what he'd accidentally done.

REFUGE

"I killed him! He's gonna die!" Steve screamed over and over again.

The police knocked on our door and informed my mom and dad of the accident. Immediately, my mom fell to her knees and cried.

"God! Dear God!" she shouted, her hands raised to the sky. "God! Save him! God, please! Save my son! I promise, I'll give you my life! Just save my son!"

"I'll never call him another name!" my dad said over and over as he offered his own promise that he had hoped would save his son.

I just stood there, watching it all happen. I could not speak. There were no words for the pain, the suffering and the bloodshed that day.

Medics rushed Jeremy to the hospital, where my parents were given little hope that he might survive.

"We are taking him into surgery now, but his injuries are severe. We don't know that he'll make it, and even if he does, the spread of the bullet has likely severed his spine, and he'll probably never walk again," the doctor told my parents.

When the doctor left the room, my parents continued to crumble.

I do not remember my parents consoling each other. If my dad had tried, my mom probably would have rejected him. In that moment, knowing her son might die, I think the nonsense of her life with him was a nonsense she could no longer tolerate.

That day could have been my brother's last, but

Jeremy came through surgery. The bullet had missed his spine by an eighth of an inch.

"I don't know how it's possible, but his spine is completely intact," the doctor told us. "He's likely to make a full recovery."

And he did.

Within a month, Jeremy was home. The Sunday following his return, Mom had all of us kids in church. She went forward at the end of the service and held her hands up to God and cried, thanking God for saving her son and keeping her promise. That day, she gave her life to God, and almost instantly, life as we'd known it started to change.

My dad went back to his evil ways and wasted no time telling Jeremy what a no-good excuse for a kid he was, quickly abandoning his promise never to say a bad word to him again.

But my mom meant business. Her promise to God was absolute. She began volunteering at our local Nazarene church and gave herself and her kids over to God in a big way. As her ties to the church grew stronger, so did her unwillingness to accept more mistreatment from my dad, his father, his brothers and their sons. Although it took three years after Jeremy's accident, she eventually kicked my dad out of the house.

My dad lost his hold on her and, as a result, lost his hold on the rest of us. She'd grown tired of the life they had been living and the abuse we all suffered, and she'd grown strong enough to make him leave us alone.

REFUGE

There were no words for us kids when they divorced. No discussion. No explanation. But there was peace, just like the times he'd spent a night or two in jail for beating my mom — only, this time, we didn't fear he'd return.

The local Nazarene church became our refuge — the same church had given us food and shelter years before, but we'd abandoned it in the middle of the night, unable to afford their generosity.

Without questions, the church welcomed us back, forgiving any fault of my mom for the choices she'd made when in a situation with few options. The church became our family, and my mom found her place in it, cleaning it every single week in an effort to show her appreciation for the kindness they showed us and raising her hands to God the rest of the week for the forgiveness and fresh start he had bestowed upon her.

Many times, I stood next to my mom during worship in church and watched how openly she spoke to God. In song. In prayer. In everything she did, she praised God. All of her angst fell away. I did not need to understand *how* God set her free to know that she was following him, and I would follow her wherever she led. I felt safe for the first time in my life, and I knew no more harm would be done to us. She would make sure of that.

This was not my first experience in church or learning about God. As a young child, I'd gone to church with neighbors and sometimes by myself. God's love was not a new idea, but I hadn't always believed it was available to me. When the abuse by my relatives began, continued and then escalated, I questioned why God did not protect me. I wondered if God really loved me if he didn't save me in my time of enormous need.

Still, even as a very young child, something inside me always yearned for a better life than the life I was living or the life my mom had tolerated for herself and, as a result, for the rest of us.

As we grew up and left home one by one, each one of us struggled in our own way to make sense of our childhood experiences. Whether it was looking for comfort in multiple relationships, drugs or a bottle, we each tried to cope with our past.

What I wanted most and prayed for was a good man I could trust. Even as a child, I knew I wanted to marry a man who was honest and hardworking and would love me and treat me well for the rest of my life. When I met my husband, he was all of those things, and I was grateful to God for the gift of him.

We lived just 100 yards from my mom, and she was part of my everyday life. We took a walk together every day, and I observed her strength and progress. She was no longer on welfare, she worked a full-time job to provide for herself and still cleaned the church every week as part of her service to God. She was a woman of promise who had kept her promise, and I loved her even more for it.

My dad never fully disappeared. He was still around, and so was my grandpa. My mom had such a forgiving heart that years after the agony my sisters and I suffered from Grandpa, when he was no longer able to take care of himself, she allowed him to live in a back room of her house, and she helped take care of him. When I saw him as an old, wrinkled, weak white-haired man, I started to forgive him, too. Everything he had done to us was between him and God. I chose not to wallow in it and let it go.

My dad came around to visit his dad, and my mom let him. When he was down on his luck and needed a place to stay, my mom let him sleep in the back room with my grandpa — until my dad got too comfortable and tried to act like he owned the place.

"Get out, Rick," she would tell him. "You're not my husband anymore. It's time for you to go."

My dad learned there was no point in arguing with my mom because she no longer tolerated it, so he would leave and come back after things cooled off. When he returned, my mom let him hang around until he inevitably crossed her well-defined boundaries again, then she sent him on his way. It was a dance they had both accepted, with my mom in the lead.

The truth is, my dad never stopped loving my mom and wanted to be near her. We all saw it, but my mom paid no attention to what he wanted other than to allow him to visit his own father in her home.

My mom never earned more than minimum wage but built herself a lovely life, taking pride in paying her own rent and saving enough money to pay cash for everything she owned, including her car.

She did not have much, but she was rich in the ways

that mattered most to her — she was free, and so were her children.

There came a time when my mom slowed down, when the routine weekly task of cleaning the church became too difficult for her. She was short of breath and not feeling well, but her doctors were having a hard time diagnosing what was causing her demise.

The day before she was scheduled for a routine test to help rule out or diagnose presumed ulcers, she took the 100-yard walk from her house to mine. Usually, she spent a few minutes or even an hour visiting, but this time she stayed several hours.

My daughter had been sick, and when I put her down for a nap, I remember thinking, *Mom, please go home so I can take a nap.* But she stayed the rest of the afternoon.

The next day, after her scheduled procedure, she had a hard time coming out of the anesthesia. Every time she started to wake up, she began vomiting. Even though she was not doing well and was at the hospital, she was only scheduled for an outpatient procedure, so the doctor was anxious to release her.

"You need to take her home," the doctor insisted. "She can't stay here any longer."

"I'm not taking her home," I insisted. "She is sick, and she is not leaving this hospital!"

Within a couple hours, the doctor released her to the emergency room. Two hours later, she was admitted to the intensive care unit. Two hours after that, she was dead.

She had died of cardiomyopathy. The technician who

assessed her heart said she had never seen a heart so worn out and was shocked that she'd gone undiagnosed for so long.

During the minutes before she died, I stayed at her side and kept telling her how much I loved her. I held her hand and tried to settle her as she struggled to breathe.

"Mom, are you ready to go?" I asked.

She nodded. She was at peace.

When my mom died, it was one of the most difficult times of my life, and yet, it was also one of the most beautiful.

I'd known that God loved me, but the strength he gave me during the moments, days and weeks after my mom's death showed me just how much. Truly, I cannot imagine how I would have gotten through losing my mom without God's love and devotion to my healing. God's blessings began with that extra day with my mom when she stayed and visited all afternoon. And I later found comfort realizing that the timing of her routine test allowed her to be in a hospital and made comfortable in her final hours of life. She suffered less and did not die alone.

❧❧❧

My dad had been in and out of the hospital for several months before my mom died. He had been diagnosed with cirrhosis of the liver and told to quit drinking or it would kill him. He quit for a while, but he went off the deep end after Mom died.

THE CHOICE OF JOY

Dad's binge drinking led to his final visit to the hospital. It became obvious that he was not going to survive, so my siblings and I took turns visiting him at the hospital.

One evening, when it was nearing my turn to visit, my brother called me from the hospital.

"Dad is in a coma now," he explained. "There's no need for you to come today. The doctors said it could go on for days, but he won't come out of it."

The next morning, my dad unexpectedly woke up from his coma, and the first thing he did was ask a nurse to call Pastor Mike at my church and ask him to come there right away.

I never asked my dad what had happened to him when he was in the coma.

I only know that when Pastor Mike arrived at the hospital, my dad prayed with him and asked God to forgive him for his sins. Then Dad asked God into his heart and cried tears of true remorse for the life he'd lived and the pain he'd caused us all. Then my dad asked Pastor Mike to go to the Christmas performance that night at the church and tell me about what he had done.

The next night, I went to see my dad at the hospital. I'd been so busy with the Christmas program at church that I almost did not go, but I felt like it was the right thing to do for my dad.

It was a visit like no other we ever had. From the moment I walked in, it was obvious he needed to share with me what was on his heart. I was more than willing to receive it, but I had never expected to hear such words coming from my dad.

"I need you to know that I am proud of you, Sarah," my dad told me for the first time without being falling-down drunk. "I need you to know how much I love you."

This was a different man before me. The person my whole family had feared was a puddle of tears, begging my forgiveness for the years of damage he'd done.

During our three-hour visit, my dad kept repeating how sorry he was for the hurt he had caused us all.

"How can God forgive me? How can he forgive my sins? I've done so many terrible things." He went on and on. "I never told your mom how much I loved her and how sorry I was. How can God forgive me? I don't deserve his forgiveness."

"God's love and forgiveness is free," I assured him. "It is there for all of us truly seeking it."

As his tears settled and he tired enough to drift off to sleep, I told him once again that I loved him. Then I left the hospital for home, certain of God's love for me and recognizing the time I'd just spent with my dad was a gift God meant for me to receive.

The next morning, Dad slipped into a coma again.

When I left him that night, I recalled things my mom told me about him as a young man, when they first met. She said he had a brilliant mind and could fix anything. The way she spoke of him matched nothing I knew or observed firsthand, except for this: She told me that from the time they met, he was drunk with his dad and brothers by 9 in the morning. She said they'd been cruel and tortured souls from the start. Even then, my mom must have known the life she would lead with him, although I doubt she could have imagined just how horrific it would be.

My dad's stay in the hospital continued without any change. Three days after my extended visit with him, a woman I hardly knew approached me at church.

"I feel like there is something I need to pray with you about," she told me.

I was a bit taken aback by her statement.

"Is there somewhere we can go to pray together?" she asked.

I agreed to pray with her, and the two of us walked into a private room where I felt comfortable sharing openly with her about my dad.

"I just want to pray that God has mercy on my dad and to not let him linger for a long time," I cried. "And I don't want him to die alone."

I knew his coma could go on for days and days, and he might die when none of us could be with him. I did not want him to die alone and wanted one of us to be with him, as I had been able to be with our mom.

I soon left the church and went to the hospital with my oldest sister, Amy. When we arrived in my dad's room, he was barely breathing.

"Can you tell me anything about my dad today?" I asked a nearby nurse.

"Your dad probably won't survive the hour," she

explained. "If you want others to come say their goodbyes, you'd better get them here now."

I immediately went back to my dad's room to tell Amy.

"Amy, the nurse said Dad will probably die within the hour, so we need to call everyone and get them here," I frantically told her.

"I think Dad is dying right now!" Amy said. "He doesn't have an hour!"

I stopped thinking about calling anyone else and just concentrated on what my dad needed.

I got on one side of the bed, and Amy got on the other.

For several days, he'd made no movement. He'd not responded to our voices or our attempts to get him to acknowledge we were with him. He'd been lifeless.

I held one of his hands, and Amy held the other.

Miraculously, he barely opened his eyes and moved his head slightly to look at each of us one last time. He knew we were there.

My sister Amy had struggled with my dad over the years. She was the one who'd suffered the most abuse at his hands, beginning with his attempt to molest her. Yet she stood there, holding his hand, telling him she loved him.

"It's okay, Dad. I love you. Just let go," she said. "Jesus is waiting for you."

A brief second later, he opened his eyes even wider, looked straight ahead, then closed his eyes and died.

It was that quick.

THE CHOICE OF JOY

I immediately felt gratitude for God's love. He had swiftly answered my prayer that my dad not suffer and that he not die alone. It was no mistake that Amy was the daughter with him as he took his final breath. The last moments she spent with him brought her peace in the times ahead, as she learned to forgive our dad as we believed God had also forgiven him.

❧❧❧

The death of my parents within two months of each other took its toll on me. My mom had been a part of my everyday life all of my life. I was 27 years old, and she'd been my best friend. I drew strength from her, and without her, I felt lost and alone and terribly unhappy.

There came a time when the grief became too much and began to affect my ability to mother my own daughter and happily share my life with the family and husband God had so graciously provided me.

"I need help," I finally told my husband. "I am looking to you for my happiness, and it's a burden you shouldn't have to bear."

Instead of trying to fix me or blame me for the obvious shortcomings I revealed to him in our marriage, he just loved me through it. I started counseling and got the help I needed.

In my struggle to understand what happened to me in childhood, I questioned how God could have let me endure such suffering.

REFUGE

After months of counseling and time spent in prayer, asking God to lead me to understanding, I began to realize that in my suffering, God suffered alongside me. My childhood was not what God wanted for me. It was not his desire that I be molested or that I watch my mom be beaten to the floor at the hands of my father. These things had nothing to do with God's love for me but had everything to do with his willingness to love me through it.

I worked through the agony of my past and learned, in time, that joy is a choice. It is waiting for all of us if only we are willing to receive it. With these things in mind, I pressed forward toward the joyful life I'd always wanted. I accepted the good and the bad that made me who I was and wanted to be.

It would take each of my siblings time to find peace in his or her own way. My two youngest sisters, Tammy and Kathy, struggled the most and had been living with my mom when she died. Although they didn't suffer sexual abuse, largely because of their young ages when Mom moved us all out, my father was still mentally and physically abusive long after the sexual abuse ended.

Tammy and Kathy had never lived outside of my mother's home and did not adjust well on their own. They ended up losing their jobs and the few possessions they owned because they could not pay their bills. They got caught in a vicious cycle of drugs and alcohol before my other sisters and my two brothers and I caught on. They took turns calling one of us for gas money and another for grocery money, then spent it all on partying without any of us realizing it.

Finally, we all figured it out and told them we would only buy them food. We cut them off from receiving any money from us.

I worried about my baby sisters, as I know my mom had. They were lost without my mom in a different way than I'd been lost without her. I leaned on God to get me through the grief, as well as my husband, but they only had each other, and neither one of them knew what to do or how to get past it. That is, until they received the nudge they needed.

Kathy woke up from a dream that changed everything for herself and Tammy. When she told me about it, I saw God at work in our family again.

"I had a dream about Mom last night. She asked me why I haven't given my life to God yet," Kathy explained.

She became very emotional about it and felt overcome by the idea that our mom was still waiting on her to find God and let him into her life.

"I told Mom that I didn't want to do it alone. I told her I was waiting for Tammy."

In the dream, Mom calmly said to her, "Is that what you are going to tell Christ when you stand before him, that you were waiting on Tammy?"

That night at church, both Kathy and Tammy promised their lives to Jesus. Together, they did what my mom would have been praying for them to do had she still been alive.

REFUGE

༒༒༒

Many times since my mom died, I've had a recurring dream about her.

We are at our church home, Ridgefield Church of the Nazarene, and my mom is suddenly standing next to me. She is worshiping God just as she had always done, with her hands lifted to him and her eyes closed as she prayed and shed tears over her love for him.

Even though I know in my dream that my mom has died, it feels completely natural to worship God next to her in church.

"Yes, sweet Jesus. Oh, how I love you, Jesus," my mom cries.

"Mom?"

The pastor is preaching the word of God, and my mom is receiving the words with an open heart, allowing the blessings of Jesus to penetrate her soul.

"Yes, Sarah?" she answers.

"Oh, Mom! It's so good to see you at church today!"

In the dream, only I can see her.

She is wearing the dress she wore at my wedding — the same dress we buried her in — and she is standing before me as if she belongs there, as if she is alive and praising God the way she'd always done.

When church is over, we walk together to the foyer and hug goodbye.

"Mom, I'm so glad you came to church today."

THE CHOICE OF JOY

We release our embrace, and she looks into my eyes, placing her hands on my cheeks.

"I'm glad I came, too."

ॐ ॐ ॐ

It's been many years since my mom and dad died. She's been gone half my life, but not a day goes by when I do not think of them and know that, despite our struggles, the life we lived as children and have overcome as adults is a testament to the possibilities available with God through his love for each of us.

I chose God as a child. My mom chose God when my brother almost died. My father chose God on his deathbed.

My mom used to say about my dad, "You watch, that old coot is going to wait until he's on his deathbed and slide under the door to heaven."

That appears to be exactly what he did. Had he found God sooner, he might have lived his last years in peace, showing love to his children and maybe even my mother. Instead, he suffered for a lifetime, then found peace and forgiveness in a hospital bed in the final days of his life. I do not wish that on anyone, and yet, I am grateful God is always calling to us, all the way until our final breath.

All these years later — my own daughter now grown, my husband and I celebrating decades together as a thriving married couple — I still believe that joy is a choice. How we get to it varies. All that matters, in the end, is that we get to it.

AN UNLIKELY FAIRY TALE
THE STORY OF RICCI AND JACK
WRITTEN BY KAREN KOCZWARA

I'm just here to do the deal. Get rid of the meth.

I stared at the guy before me — long, wild, curly hair; bare chest; pale, skinny.

He looks like a lion, I mused. *A very scary lion.*

I felt his eyes on me as we exchanged our goods. *He's sizing me up, taking me in.*

"We should be together, you know that?" he blurted.

I stared at him, surprised at his boldness. *What did he just say?*

He kept pressing, insisting.

Who does this guy think he is?

I would soon find out. The pale, skinny guy with the crazy hair was about to step into my life, and things would never be the same.

భవించ

Ricci

I was born in 1974 to two young kids — a girl of Mexican descent and a redheaded Irish boy. Not ready to raise a child, they gave me up for adoption. My adoptive mother, who'd struggled with infertility, learned of the pregnancy from her best friend, and two weeks after my birth, she and my father brought me home. My mother was elated — a child of her own, at last! It was the beginning of what could have been a happily ever after, but my life better resembled the darker segments of storybook fairy tales.

From a very early age, I sensed something was amiss in our home. My father, 17 years my mother's senior, had been married twice before and had several children from the previous relationships. An angry man, he yelled and drank a lot. As a young child, I sat in a highchair and watched him hurl a glass of milk at my mother in a fit of rage. It was my earliest memory of his violence. Many similar, terrible scenes followed.

My mother, a naïve, soft-spoken woman, became powerless under my father's angry grip. She returned to school to finish her teaching degree, and my father often watched me. Though I did not recall his molestation (and still don't), I began acting out what he'd done to me, too young and innocent to understand the horror of it all. Years later, I would learn of the allegations from other girls he'd hurt, and my heart would sink to the floor.

When I turned 5, we moved to a small town in Northern Washington, settling in just before the infamous eruption of the volcano Mount St. Helens. We lived on a farm, and I instantly fell in love with our new home. With ample space to run, play, jump and get dirty, it was paradise for a young tomboy like me. Green trees dotted the open land, and acres of fields served as home to the livestock we raised. While I spent much of my time alone, the dogs and cows became my best friends. From afar, everything seemed postcard perfect. But up close, things looked much different. The nightmare that had begun in our old house had followed us to our new town.

My mother landed a teaching job in town, and I spent much of the day helping my father on the farm. My father often drank on the job, lugging his beer with him into the field. On one particularly hot day, when I was 6, I accompanied my dad up the mountain to work with our cows in the pasture there. As the sun beat down on our heads, I grew especially thirsty. My father had forgotten to pack me a drink, so he handed me his beer. I winced as the cold liquid trickled down my throat, not especially fond of the taste. It would be the first of many more sips to come.

By 7 years old, I'd learned the drill. The more my father drank, the angrier he became. After nursing his beer all day in the fields, he often wandered down to the local bar, where he drank some more. When he stumbled home, he lashed out at my mother and me, his harsh words bouncing off the walls and piercing our ears. My mother, exhausted from a long day's work, slipped into her pajamas the minute she walked in the door and retreated to her room. She became depressed and slept much of the time, trying to drown out the monotony and the terror. I watched from afar, and hopelessness crept into my chest. I began to hate the booze, because it turned my father into a monster. To bleed out my anger, I began whipping the trees with cow whips, watching as the lashes made indentations in the bark. One time I even killed a six-pack of beer with a hatchet, just because I didn't want Dad to drink it. *How much longer could we all keep going on this way,* I wondered, *herding cattle and hiding our pain?*

School was not a pleasant escape. As a chubby, stubborn and troubled little girl, I was often deemed a nuisance in class. My kindergarten teacher repeatedly sent me into the closet when I made mischief, and I peered through the glass French doors, counting the minutes until the bell rang. In first grade, my parents sent me to school with a letter, granting permission for my teachers to hit me if I misbehaved. The teacher even made me wear a paper seatbelt so I would not jump out of my chair. My grades, which I'd kept up at first, began to suffer. With the constant mistreatment at home, I no longer cared about spelling or math. My behavior surely disappointed my mother, who taught one door down from my classroom and who scrambled to salvage her reputation. We were both victims in our own right, both silently wearing our shame, trudging through each day in hopes the next one might be better somehow.

My parents split up and reconciled frequently. My mother and I went to stay with relatives until she and my father worked things out. I was tossed back and forth, not sure when to pack my things and when to settle in. My world became a frightening, unpredictable tornado of confusion and pain. The minute one storm finally calmed, another one blew in.

By age 9, I began experimenting with boys, kissing the

neighbor boy in our barn after school. I was desperate for attention of any sort and did not care how I got it. My father's cruelty escalated, and he reminded me of a raging monster. While I'd once enjoyed tagging along with him in the field, I now feared for my safety. One day, I took my cousins out to the barn during calving season. This act was especially dangerous, and when my father learned what I'd done, he lashed out, picking me up by my ankles and hitting me with his belt. The metal prong became lodged in my leg, and I yelped in pain. It was a lesson I'd never forget.

On another occasion, my father drank so much out in the field, he decided he could not get home on the horse. So he hopped in the truck, and I hopped on the horse instead. Once Dad was gone, the horse started to act up and took off at a dead run. Instead of waiting to fall off once we hit the gravel, I decided to let myself fall off in the field. My body and head hit hard. Exasperated by the horse's behavior, my father hooked the horse up to his pickup and dragged it down the road behind him until the horse collapsed and couldn't get back up again. I watched in horror. Though the poor animal lived, the awful image remained imprinted in my mind for years.

My father often promised to stop drinking, but he never followed through.

"I'll just drink beer in the evenings," he vowed. I wanted to believe him, but before noon the next day, he'd already have polished off a few beers.

My mother kept up the best she could, never talking

back to my father despite her weary state. Yet my father could find insult where none had been intended. One evening, after she whipped up a simple meal of macaroni and cheese and wienies, my father looked at her with disgust, irritated by her choice of words.

"This is a junk meal!" he cried. "I can't eat this stuff!" He pushed back his plate and headed out to the bar, where he drank until the early hours of the morning.

My neighbors, sympathetic to my plight, took me to Sunday school with them. I enjoyed church, but I wasn't sure what I thought of God or what he might think of me. My father didn't much like me going to church, but he didn't try to stop me.

"Those folks are just a bunch of Bible thumpers," he muttered.

I ignored his remarks. In a sea of uncertainty and hardship, Sunday school was a pleasant escape, a place to forget all about my troubles at home.

Often, my father wandered into my room in a drunken stupor and screamed at me after I'd gone to bed. "You little slut! You don't love me!" I huddled under the covers, heart thumping so loudly I feared he could hear it from the doorway. To protect myself from him, I began sleeping with my mother. Her warmth comforted me. With two bodies in the bed, we were a small army, and we stood a better chance against his rage.

The next morning, my father might return to his cheerful self, teaching me all about cows and driving. But before long, his violence flared up again, and he took out his rage on me and the animals. When our dogs refused to work, he choked them and shoved manure down their mouths. I cried as I tried to stop him, horrified as the dogs yelped in protest. No being, it seemed, was safe when my father started drinking.

One chilly January night, my father stumbled into the house especially late. My mother climbed out of bed to go to the bathroom. After he mumbled some nonsense, Mom told him to just go pass out.

"You've been waiting for this for a long time!" my father snarled.

Moments later, he returned, this time with his 30-30 hunting rifle. As he attempted to load it, my mother jumped up and tackled him to the ground with her panties still around her ankles. Panicked, I ran for the phone.

"Ricci's going to call the cops!" my mother screamed.

My father turned in his rage and ripped the phones out of the walls. Adrenaline surged through my veins, and I ran for the neighbor's house, my bare feet splashing through the cracked ice puddles my father's truck had driven through just minutes before. I raced to the neighbor's back door, and to my amazement, the moment I banged on it, it miraculously opened.

"He's gonna kill her!" I screamed as I raced into the house.

The rest of the night progressed like a slow-motion nightmare. I watched, eyes wide, as my father stepped into the back of a cop car a while later and rode off into the dark. I went to stay at a friend's house and refused to come home until he was gone for good. But just as it seemed possible to hope for normalcy and peace, my father returned. Over an ice cream cone, he informed me he and my mother were going to work things out.

"Well, you can do it alone, because I can't do this anymore," I snapped. Though just 12 years old, I was done dealing with the madness. If my mother took my father back, I didn't know what I would do. I refused to spend the rest of my life hiding under the covers, wondering when his wrath would strike again.

My mother mustered the courage to leave, filed for divorce and moved us into town. We left many of our things behind, never to be seen again. At last, we could sleep well at night.

Though we'd turned the page into another chapter, life didn't get any easier. I took advantage of my mother's weakness and began partying hard, messing around with boys and drinking. I met a boy visiting from Spokane. After partying with him and his friends at his parents' cabin, I got especially drunk and lost my virginity to him. The next morning, I awoke, hung over and overwhelmed. Had I really just given my body over to a total stranger? It hardly mattered at that point. I was already too broken, too beaten down from life — vulnerable and shattered from the inside out.

The next couple years became a blur of drugs, drinking and partying. I cared nothing about school or my grades. Though not a popular girl, I longed to be accepted. By 14, I began drinking at least three days a week, often bragging about how many beers I could put down. I lost some weight, and boys and men began paying me more attention. For once, I felt good about myself. *I'm finally getting noticed. This is what I've always wanted, isn't it?*

The drunken nights muddled together. I often awoke half naked, certain I'd been taken advantage of after blacking out. *Well, you asked for it, didn't you, Ricci? You drank too much and let those guys misuse you.* I tossed my heart out the window, along with any feeling that went with it. What did it matter if I slept with a hundred boys?

My friends and I began playing with black magic, including a Ouija board. It seemed harmless at first — even fun.

After we scared a neighbor boy half to death, his mother spoke to the pastor of the church she and my mother attended. He showed up on our doorstep one day, wanting to pray over our house. Uncomfortable with his approach, my mother stopped going to church after that.

Another friend invited me to church, and I agreed to go. I had enjoyed Sunday school as a kid and hoped I might like it still. As I sat in the pew, the pastor discussed the youth of our society and the trouble we got ourselves into.

"This rock and roll music is especially a problem," he warned. "Many of the lyrics contain subliminal messages, and our children are practicing magic!"

My friend gently took my hand and led me to the front of the room, where someone prayed over me. Embarrassed, I half listened, not interested in this God they talked about. *If God does exist, he must hate me to have given me a crummy life like this,* I thought bitterly.

My best friend from first grade took me to her church as well. I especially enjoyed the entertainment aspect. When the youth leaders called for a game of flashlight hide-and-seek in the dark, I took advantage of the opportunity to kiss boys in the corner. I moved in with my friend for a brief time, and we began partying and smoking cigarettes together. When our parents learned we'd been up to no good, I took the blame. It seemed no matter where I went, trouble always followed.

By 15, I was harder to control than ever before. Desperate to maintain her respectable reputation as a schoolteacher in a small town, my mother did what she had to do. She placed me in a foster home to keep me safe from harm. The police removed me from school one day and took me home to pack, and I left for my new home. But the arrangement didn't last long. I ran away twice, winding up on the streets for two weeks before my mother at last relented and let me move home. That same year, my father remarried. It should have been a fresh start for all of us, a chance to make things right and begin again. But I was a wrecking ball now, crashing into everything in my path. The past abuse had taken its toll, and I was a destructive, hurting girl. Life was about to get even harder.

At 16, I no longer wanted to live. I attempted suicide by cutting my wrists, desperate to escape my pain. After getting kicked out of three schools in three months, I dropped out and opted to get my GED. One night, my mother came home to find me naked and beat up in the front yard, the traumatic result of too much hard partying with dangerous characters.

"Do you want help, Ricci? You need real help," she told me.

She sent me to a treatment program, and after 34 days, I completed my time and came home. But that night, instead of staying in and staying sober, I got drunk again. The destructive cycle continued.

The next two years became a fog of more drinking, promiscuity and suicidal thoughts and attempts. I landed my first job as a waitress and moved into an apartment with a fellow employee. I hated waitressing, and many of my customers gave me a hard time because I was not Hispanic like them and messed up their orders because I couldn't understand them. When the money ran low, I considered applying for food stamps, but I didn't have a clue where to even ask for an application. Drugs and alcohol dominated my life, and I cared about little else. After quitting my waitressing job, I landed another job at a local hotel. One day, hung over from drinking too much the night before, I threw up in the sink of a hotel room just before cleaning it. I watched the vomit swirl down the drain, disgusted by who I'd become. *Is this it? Is this really all there is to life?*

In the fall of 1993, I met a cute boy at a carnival in Walla Walla. I had messed around with plenty of boys, but I'd never been in love before. This time, it was different. The moment I laid eyes on him, I could hardly peel them away. *This guy is something special,* I thought, hardly able to breathe.

"I'm Ricci." I introduced myself, feeling my face flush.

"Brent," he replied with a smile.

Weak-kneed, heart thumping, I smiled back.

Not long after we began dating, he moved home with his mother in Newberg, Oregon. I got a bus ticket and followed him there immediately, determined to make a life with him. I landed a job working nights at a nursing home, and he found work at a local Burger King.

At first, all seemed blissful. We drank here and there, and he introduced me to meth, which his mother and her boyfriend used. Before long, the drug sucked me in. I loved the high, the way it allowed me to stay up for days, feeling as if I was invincible. For a while, life felt steady and good. I had a new love, a new drug and a new job in a new town. I was going to be okay.

And then one morning, all hell broke loose. I returned home from work to find Brent's mother frantic and angry. She'd run out of drugs, and she was not happy. "Why isn't the floor vacuumed?" she screamed, storming around the house. Her eyes bore into mine, and I jumped back. Paranoid, I burst into tears and fled to Burger King, where I told Brent about his mother's rage.

"We gotta get out of there before she blows her top," he agreed.

I grabbed my two pet rats and a few other belongings, and we headed back to my town and rented a studio house. The drinking, drugs and partying continued. I cheated on Brent, and he cheated on me. After he walked out, I lost my mind, completely broken and lost. I cut my wrists and went crazy and, eventually, spent time in a psych ward at a mental hospital. Next, after getting caught for having weed, I landed in jail. After getting out, the court ordered treatment for me at a facility in Yakima. The treatment turned out to be a genuinely helpful program. At last, I had some tools to help me get back on track. But not long after finishing the program, I slipped back into my old ways. I could not kick my meth habit, and life felt bleak and dark.

My best friend, who'd gotten pregnant young and married shortly after, called me one day, distraught. Her new husband had been diagnosed with a brain tumor. I reeled from the news. Nine months later, she showed up at my door, her face streaked with tears.

"My baby's gone, Ricci. Gone," she cried.

I threw my arms around my friend, and we sobbed together, grieving the loss. I was high, as usual, and wished for once I wasn't. I could not find the words to comfort my friend, so we simply held each other until the tears dried up.

The tragedy rattled me, but not enough to prompt me to clean up my life. Meth kept me in its grip, as did booze. I drifted in and out of houses, always getting kicked out when the money dried up or I caused trouble. My best friend looked after me, making sure I had a place to sleep and enough food to eat. I attempted suicide several more times, taking pills and slitting my wrists. If a gun had showed up at the house, I surely would have shot myself in the head. After waking up in the hospital after my suicide attempts, I would lean back against the pillow, my insides filling with dread and despair. *Why am I still here?* Anger toward the doctors and toward God flooded me. *Couldn't they have just let me die? Who would miss a screwed-up girl like me?*

My mother, who had remarried, grew tired of seeing me in such desperate situations. She bought me a pickup truck and a fifth-wheel trailer to live in. I met another guy, and within no time, he began beating me. I grew afraid of him, often hitting back. When the cops showed up at our place, they asked if I wanted to press charges.

"No, just get him away from me," I begged.

I had hit another low point. My 21st birthday came and went, and I begged to go back to treatment. I got clean for almost eight months, setting a personal record. I reconnected with my sisters from my father's previous marriage. One of my sisters, Jennifer, had just gotten busted for drugs and lost her two children to the foster system. The older sister, Cassie, took me in and helped me get back on my feet. A family friend offered me a job as a quality control inspector at a company in Vancouver. I accepted the job, and for the first time in a long while, I felt good about myself. *Maybe things are about to take a turn for the better now. I'll put my past behind me and start over here. Surely, life will improve.*

I moved in with my new boss, and she took good care of me. After buying myself a truck, my pride swelled. I was now officially drug free, but I could not give up the booze, and I drank regularly on the weekends. After a year, life had taken on a happy, predictable pace. *I'm really making it now! I'm a new person, healthy and happy at last!*

And then, another bomb dropped. My boss became dissatisfied with her pay and decided to leave the job, me and our place behind. Unable to afford rent on my own, I moved in with another co-worker. It didn't take long to learn the ugly truth — my new roommates were also meth addicts. Had I managed to find the only meth heads in our drug-free company? After getting messed up with them, I lost my job and wound up back on the streets, right back where I'd begun.

I met a new guy at a bar, and he took me in. We used drugs together.

"You should go back home and ask your mom for money," he told me.

I agreed to the plan and talked my mother into giving me some money, but my new boyfriend took it all from me, leaving me completely dry. I'd foolishly trusted him, and now I was penniless once again. My mother had my trailer back home, so I moved into a dingy mobile home. With no electricity and rusty water trickling from the sink, the place was nothing but a dirty drug house. I'd hit another low, but there seemed no way out. *This is just my life. From one drug house to the next, one deal after another, hopping between couches, scrambling for meals, always high. I just can't seem to escape the cycle, even when I try.*

REFUGE

I went on a drug deal with one of my many roommates one day. When we got there we went in, and on the couch sat a pale, skinny guy with long, wild hair. He did not have a shirt on and was unkempt from head to toe. *That guy looks like a scary lion,* I mused.

The guy stared at me as we exchanged our goods. "We should be together," he blurted.

I stared back at him. *Is he crazy? What is he talking about?*

I learned the lion's name — Jack. Druggies called him Doctor Jack, as he used needles and often helped folks find a vein when they had killed all the regular ones. We began hanging out.

Jack continued to express interest, but I assured him he didn't want to mess with me. "I'm messed up in the head," I told him.

Jack smiled. "Me, too."

Beyond the crazy hair and the disheveled look, there was something appealing about this lion-like guy. He was funny, and instinctively, I trusted him. Unlike the other guys I'd dated, who'd run off with my money or with other women, I felt pretty sure Jack would never hurt me if I turned my heart over to him. *Maybe I should give him a chance. We're both messed up, and I don't have anywhere else to go.*

Trying reverse psychology, I started bugging him to shoot me up.

"NO! I don't want to do that to you," Jack insisted.

"Well, it's good enough for you," I would argue. Truly

AN UNLIKELY FAIRY TALE

I was scared of needles and wanted no part of it, but as usual, my big mouth and stubborn streak backed us both into a corner, and he finally gave in. That night, I entered a whole other world.

Before long, Jack and I became a couple, intertwining our dysfunctional lives in a thick, tangled web of drugs and darkness. But we hadn't even reached the scariest part of our storybook fairy tale. We were about to embark on a journey that could plunge us into even more treacherous waters. And if we did not grab onto a lifeline and pull ourselves to shore, it might be too late for both of us.

ॐॐॐ

In fairy tales, the knight in shining armor always rides up on the white horse, swoops up the girl and whisks her off into the sunset. I'd like to say this was the case for Jack and me, that I'd found my Prince Charming at last. But the truth was that we were both two junkies who came together and tried to make it work. And for a long time, it was very, very hard.

Like me, Jack had endured a hard life, filled with drugs, booze, rock and roll and a string of broken relationships. As a child, he'd endured abuse from several stepfathers and was taunted by his peers for wetting his pants. As a teenager, he'd developed into a reckless kid, picking fights, stirring up trouble with the law and always looking for the next adrenaline rush. Jack had three children with two different women. He'd lived life in the fast lane for a very long time and had no intention of slowing down anytime soon.

Jack landed a great job in Portland, making the long drive from our home to work every day. In 1997, we moved to Portland, telling no one but our mothers. We started getting clean, determined to get off drugs for good.

I loved Jack — the way he made me laugh, the way he protected me. I knew no matter what came my way, he'd always have my back. But the alcohol and drugs kept getting in the way, and in between the good times, we fought often.

Sometimes, things got so ugly, I threw his stuff out the window. Our landlord tried to evict us several times, but Jack always smoothed things over with him. I knew we could not keep up the charade. If we did not clean up our act, we'd surely fall apart.

"We have to make a choice," I told Jack. It was time for a change. We were both tired of the lifestyle. Years of drug abuse, drinking, partying and fighting had taken a toll on both of us, physically and emotionally. I dreamed of a sober life, one in which we went shopping at the mall, had children and dined at nice restaurants with friends. But for so long, we'd both lived in a dark, ugly world, drifting between drug houses, running from the cops, wandering from one bad relationship to the next. If we wanted things to be different, we had to make a choice to put an end to our destructive ways for good.

As the years passed, Jack and I continued living together, drinking on and off. I remembered my Sunday school days and the God I'd heard about as a child. I hadn't thought much about God in the past, convinced he didn't care much about me. I'd lashed out at him after waking up following my suicide attempts, angry to still be alive. To me, if he really did exist, he was just some guy in the sky, not someone I wanted anything to do with.

But suddenly, I could not shake the urge to go to church. *I think we're supposed to go.* The urge became stronger as the months passed.

During an exploratory surgery, a doctor confirmed what I'd suspected all along — I could not have children. I was not surprised — Jack and I had not used birth control the entire time we'd been together, and I'd never gotten pregnant.

"Your fallopian tubes are blocked at both ends," the doctor said. "I'm sorry."

I went home and cried for a long time. *I guess I'm not meant to be a mother after all.* As awful as my childhood had been, I'd always hoped to raise a child of my own someday. Would that ever happen now?

I continued to think about church. Jack wanted nothing to do with God, and I didn't blame him, in a way. Every man he'd known in his life had walked out on him. Why would God be any different?

Meanwhile, he tried to stop smoking cigarettes. Suddenly, he feared he might be dying of cancer. He developed polyps in the back of his throat and went to the doctor every few weeks to get them checked out. Quitting smoking made him angry, though, and he lashed out and hit me one night. I called the cops, and he went to jail for domestic violence. The destructive cycle continued.

On Christmas Day 2003, Jack proposed to me at my mother's house in front of nearly 30 people. As I picked up wrapping paper following the gift opening, my family said, "Sit down, Ricci. We have one more present for you." My heart did a small flip. *Is this what I think it is?*

Jack got down on one knee. "I love you, Ricci. Will you be my wife?"

I jumped up, threw my arms around him and gave him a resounding "yes."

But it wasn't happily ever after from there, either. In February the following year, we drank too much, and the night quickly went south. I ended up taking off for most of the night. He accused me of infidelity, and in the middle of our fight, I put my head through a double-paned window. Blood trickled everywhere. The cops were called, and off to the hospital I went for another 72 hours in the psych ward.

In the hospital, I had plenty of time to think. *What are we doing here? Can I really marry this guy? We love each other, but we're always fighting, and we can't stay away from the booze. If we are going to be together, we cannot go on like this anymore. One of us will wind up dead.*

"We can't drink anymore. At all," I told Jack firmly when I got home.

"I agree," Jack said. "We're done."

We never touched another drink again.

In July, my mother and I started working on wedding

plans. One day as we talked, she revealed something shocking to me. "I spent many nights on my knees praying, begging God to protect you because I knew I couldn't," she said.

Wow. All these years, my mother has been praying for me? That's really something! I knew there were plenty of times I should have wound up dead — had my mother's prayers really worked?

Jack remained concerned about his health, convinced he was dying of cancer following years of smoking. "I am ready to go back to church," he said at last. "But I only want to go to the one I went to as a kid."

As a child, Jack had watched his mother go through a string of men. She'd sent him to church as a way to get him out of her hair, and he'd found refuge there. The people were kind, unlike the harsh men in his life. Though he hadn't been in years, he'd always had fond memories of the place that once embraced him as a little boy. I was thrilled he wanted to return.

"Okay," I agreed. *Thank you, God! At last, he's ready!*

We made the nearly 18-mile drive to Ridgefield Church of the Nazarene each week, knowing the effort was well worth it. *This is where we need to be right now. After years of running and trying to do things our way, this is a step in the right direction.*

Everyone at the church was very kind. The moment we walked in the doors for the first time, a sweet lady came up to me and pulled me into a hug. *Wow, that doesn't happen every day. This feels really nice.*

When the pastor approached us and asked if we had any kids, I replied, "No, I can't have children. God has another plan for me."

"Do you know how many couples have said that same thing to me and a year or two later I see them walking down the aisle with a little bundle of joy?" he said with a smile. "We have lots of praying folks here."

As the weeks passed, church became the highlight of our week. Though I still had many questions about God, I believed without a doubt he was the missing piece in my life. I had spent years assuming he was nothing but an aloof figure who couldn't care less about my problems. But the pastor spoke about him as a loving God who wanted to be deeply involved in all aspects of our lives. With God, he said, we could experience peace, joy and hope.

I'd felt a tugging on my heart for some time, and now I knew why. I had been missing these things, trying everything else in life to make myself happy. But no amount of drugs, alcohol or sex had ever been able to fill the gaping hole in my heart. I'd been a lonely, angry girl, bleeding out my pain as I cut my wrists and popped pills. At many points in my life, death had seemed a better option than life. But now, I wanted to live. I had a fiancé and a chance to start over. Jack and I still had much to work through, but with God in our lives, we found hope and purpose.

Jack and I married in September 2004. Two weeks later, we moved into a bigger house in Vancouver so Jack's son could move in with us, but a week before we settled in, it fell through. I wondered what we'd do with all that empty space. And we were about to find out.

My sister Jennifer got in contact again and kept in touch through letters, emails and phone calls. She lived in Florida with her family and still struggled to get her life together. She had five children but had already lost custody of two of them.

One day, as we talked on the phone, she asked, "Ricci, why don't you have any kids of your own?"

"It's impossible for me to conceive," I told her, sadly relaying my medical issues. "God has another plan for me."

"I would have a baby for you," Jennifer replied sweetly. "But I already scheduled a procedure that will prevent me from getting pregnant again. Sorry about your luck."

I hung up, discouraged. *Okay, God, I choose to believe you have another plan for me. I just don't know what that is. I'm trying to make the right decisions in life, and I know I'd be a great mother if I just got the chance. I enjoy being a stepmother to Jack's kids, but I'd love to have a child of my own. Help me to trust you.*

On Christmas Day 2005, Jennifer and I spoke on the phone again. She was crying and sounded distraught. "I've been in denial for a while, but I can't be anymore. I can feel the baby moving inside me. I'm pregnant, Ricci."

"I want it!" I blurted.

Little did I know, Jennifer and her husband had already discussed giving the baby to me. Due to their financial situation, she knew she could not raise another child. She called me back a week later to confirm their decision.

"We want to give the baby up for adoption to you," Jennifer said.

My heart soared. "Really?" I could hardly breathe. It seemed too good to be true. I had briefly talked it over with Jack, and he'd agreed to it, not fully believing my stepsister would so willingly give over her baby. Now, it seemed my dreams of becoming a mother would finally be realized. Perhaps God had answered my prayers, in a strange but wonderful way!

Jennifer had an ultrasound and learned the baby was a boy. I scrambled to get ready for his birth, filling the house with every possible baby contraption I could find. I set aside a chunk of time for the big day, hoping to be present when he arrived. But seven weeks before her due date, Jennifer called early one morning, breathless on the other line.

"My water broke! The baby is on the way!"

"Oh, my gosh!" I called Jack at work. "We have to get to Florida right away! The baby is coming early!"

I jumped on the computer, frantically searching for a last-minute flight to Florida. At last, I secured seats, and Jack and I headed off, ready to meet our newborn son. The anticipation mounted as I stepped off the plane. *Will it be love at first sight? Will I make a good mother? This is all happening so fast!*

The moment I laid eyes on our son, I knew he was

meant to be mine. *He is perfect, just perfect.* I counted his little fingers and toes, marveling, my heart melting. We named him Sylvester. I could not wait to bring him home.

Five days later, the state released the baby to us, and we flew back home with our new son in our arms. I knew I'd never be able to thank Jennifer enough for giving us the greatest gift a person could bestow.

Once back home, I set up an appointment with a pediatrician. Sylvester had trouble latching onto the bottle and began losing weight. I knew he had drugs in his system, and only time would tell the effects of that. A group of friends from church came to our side, offering meals and support. When our car broke down, they helped out as well. *What would I do without these people? They are such a godsend during this time!*

Eventually, I got the hang of things, and motherhood became my ultimate joy. Holding little Sylvester in my arms, I understood unconditional love at an entirely new level. *This must be how God feels about his kids.* For the first time, I understood the depth of God's love for me, and my heart completely softened.

God, I've spent my whole life trying to do things my way. We've gotten off drugs and alcohol, wanting to make better decisions. But I now understand what it means to fully surrender to your love. Just like I've instantly fallen in love with this baby, you've loved me from the beginning. I was the one who resisted you. I thought you didn't care about a girl like me. I thought I'd messed up too many times. But the pastor talks about this thing called grace.

REFUGE

And now I get it. You sent your son to die on the cross for the wrong things I did, and you made a way for me to spend eternity with you in heaven. You simply want me to confess my sins and trust you. And I want to do just that — trust you with my whole heart. You've brought Jack and me to a wonderful church, a place where we are accepted just as we are. And you accept us just as we are, too, flaws and all. Thank you for never giving up on me.

Life fell into a happy place. I loved our church, loved God and loved being a mother. That Thanksgiving, the State of Florida ordered Jennifer to leave her home, and she lost custody of her other children. She came back to visit us, and I loved having her around. Jack and I performed in a Christmas program at church, and she came to watch. She also attended a women's tea at church with me. After each event, she left with tears in her eyes. A week before Christmas, her husband called, wanting her to come home. I dropped her off at the Greyhound bus station, my heart full of sadness.

"I love you. Take care," I said, giving her a long hug. I had no idea it would be our last embrace.

Jennifer had lived a troubled life filled with drugs, just as I had. But she had also given me the greatest gift I could have asked for — a child. She would forever hold a special place in my heart. And I hoped and prayed one day she would give her heart to God. He was the only one who could erase her pain.

In March 2007, Sylvester's adoption became final. I combined our adoption party with his first birthday party.

AN UNLIKELY FAIRY TALE

It was a beautiful day, filled with friends, family and lots of laughter. As I watched little Sly mash his fingers in his cake, my heart swelled with joy. *You've brought us so far, God. I feared I'd never have children, and you've given us a miracle. You are so good!*

The children's pastor at church pulled me aside, his face grim. "I hate to be the bearer of bad news, but I just want to warn you. I feel like you might be under Satan's attack soon."

I stared at him, trying not to let fear creep in my heart. I believed Satan was a real being, an enemy of God who sought to discourage and destroy. I believed he was the one behind the lies, the one who'd tried to get me to give up on life when I'd attempted suicide multiple times. He did not want me to live a thriving life. Was he trying to pull me down now that I'd finally gotten plugged into church and given my life over to God?

In August that year, my aunt passed away. While I was at her funeral, Jack called with some terrible news. "Jennifer's been in a bad motorcycle accident. She wasn't wearing a helmet." His voice was somber on the other line. "There's no brain activity."

By the end of the night, Jennifer's husband took her off life support. Just like that, she was gone. My heart ached. *Oh, God, she led such a troubled life, but she was such a gift! She loved reading, traveling and, most of all, her family. I will never forget her as long as I live. Thank you for that precious time you gave us at Thanksgiving.*

I continued to grieve Jennifer, unable to believe she

was gone. But her death was just the beginning of many more to follow. Within the next four years, we lost three of our pastors, my stepmother and several members of our church youth. Before my stepmother's death, we learned my father had terminal lung cancer. *Oh, God, how can we bear it all? So much loss in such a short amount of time!*

It felt as if the world was ending, crumbling at our feet. But Jack and I hung on, clinging to God as our refuge. I knew we never would have gotten through this time without the hope we had in God.

In February 2010, my father went into hospice care, and I went to visit him. It was difficult to see him in so much pain. I asked Jack to take over with Sylvester so I could help take care of my father until he passed.

My father fell into an unconscious state for two weeks, but one night, he sat up in bed, completely alert and wanting macaroni and cheese. We began discussing God and heaven.

"Babe, you stick with it," my father told me, referring to my faith.

"Dad, we will see each other again in heaven," I assured him.

"Oh, don't count on that," my father replied.

"Dad, Jesus came to earth and was nailed on a cross because he loves us. He knew we couldn't do it on our own. He wants a relationship with us. But you have to believe in him, Dad," I told him softly.

My father looked at me with sadness in his eyes. "I sure hope you're right, babe. I sure hope you're right."

AN UNLIKELY FAIRY TALE

My father had been anything but perfect. He'd even blamed me for the divorce. But he was the only father I had, and I'd loved him all along. In his later years, he quit drinking, had read the Bible and had even gotten baptized. Though I knew he still struggled with skepticism, I believed he had truly given his heart to God, and I would see him again someday.

The day my father passed away, my sister, stepmother and I sat on the living room floor in silence, waiting for representatives from the funeral home to arrive. My stepmother had gone to great lengths to find four matching bags to give each of us girls one of my father's cherished rings.

As my sister looked closer at the bags, she gasped. They had the numbers 3 and 16 printed on them. My mind drifted to the conversation Dad and I had, and one of my favorite Bible verses came to mind, John 3:16: "For God so loved the world that he gave his one and only son, that whoever believes in him shall not perish but have eternal life." We then realized something else — the date was March 16, or 3/16.

God, surely this is no coincidence. You have given me a beautiful reminder that you are here, and he is with you. What a comfort. Thank you!

On March 19, we buried my father. I went over to my best friend's house to get some fresh air after the funeral. When I saw a young girl sitting on the couch, I inquired about her.

"That's my brother's girlfriend. She just lost her 2 year

old to the state and is pregnant again." She paused. "You should go talk to her."

My heart jumped. I was emotionally and physically exhausted from my father's passing. But had God just dropped an opportunity right in my lap? I went over and talked to the girl, and to my amazement, she became open to the idea of giving her baby up for adoption to me. A week later, I called an attorney, and our quest for a second child began.

Six weeks later, after a whirlwind process, Jack and I welcomed our second son, Whitman, into the world. This time, I was present for the birth. We brought him home two days later. In just a short time, I'd gone from being childless to having two young boys. God was truly good. He had given me the desires of my heart, filling it to the brim with lots of love, laughter and happy tears. But the journey was not over yet.

෧෧෧

Jack

"Good job, Sylvester!" I called out, watching my son swing the bat as the ball came his way. He made contact and started running, and I clapped for him. *What a champ! That kid is a natural at baseball!*

Watching Sylvester play baseball was one of my greatest joys, for I knew how far he'd come. Born with drugs in his system, he'd missed quite a few milestones and had been diagnosed with autism and sensory organ disorder. Whitman had genetic cognitive delays, mixed developmental delays and sensory integration disorder. Ricci spent much of her time taking them to various appointments and therapy sessions. For her, it was a full-time job, but I knew motherhood brought her great joy. There was nothing she'd rather do with her life than care for our two precious sons.

Ricci and I remained heavily involved at Ridgefield Church of the Nazarene, and we could not love it more. We found a church full of real people just like us, folks with real everyday problems. But, like us, they also had a real faith in God. This is what united us. We loved our small group, where we shared those struggles in an intimate setting and prayed for each other. The church had been the backbone of our relationship, and I didn't know what we would have done without our second family.

We also volunteered as much as possible at the church. The church was constantly growing, and it was easy to see why. Everyone, from the head pastor to the children's ministry pastor, truly cared for the people they served. I felt God's presence every time I walked in that door, and I thanked him that he led me all the way back to the place I once visited as a child.

I credited God with blessing me with a great job, and I felt grateful to be able to provide for my family. My journey toward him was a slow process. I did not soften to him as quickly as Ricci did, but God continued to work on my heart, chipping away little by little. I attended drug and alcohol classes to get clean, but surrendering my life to Jesus Christ was really the ticket. I went from a guy who once picked fights, spent time in jail and did almost every drug on earth to one who looked forward to going to church every Sunday. I was still a work in progress, but knowing God loved me and would pick me up when I made mistakes helped me get through each day. As I told my friends, life without Jesus was no life at all. I couldn't imagine trying to do things on my own now. It simply would not work.

Guys aren't much for fairly tales — it's more of a chick thing. But I did believe this much — there is no happily ever after on this earth. Life is hard, very hard. Trials will inevitably come, and Satan will try to defeat us. However, we do have a knight in shining armor, and that is Jesus Christ. He swooped in and saved us when he died on the cross, and with him, we will find a happily ever after in heaven if we invite him into our lives. There is no one too broken or dirty for Jesus. He can fix anyone. Ricci and I are living proof of that.

I couldn't know what the future holds, but I was certain of one thing. With God, all things were possible. If I fell, he'd pick me up again. If I doubted, he'd draw me back to him. Ricci and I found that hope, joy and peace at last. We forged our own unlikely fairy tale, and it's a story I was happy to tell. Because I knew it would have a happy ending.

CONCLUSION

So often, bad news surrounds us. There's a lot of it in the world. We get pretty used to it. We get used to thinking, *This is just the way things are, the ways things are going to be.* At times we get scared, overwhelmed, weary. Our lives feel empty, and we wonder, *Is this all there is?* We work hard trying to pull things together, our schedules become manic, our reserves become depleted and the reality of life hits like a lack of oxygen. Regardless of how it happens, whether our marriages begin to fall apart, a loved one gets sick, a child rebels, a job is lost, a bankruptcy looms, a relationship ends, a dream dies, someone hurts us, we hurt someone else or we have everything we could have ever wanted and our lives simply feel empty, we know we can't keep going on like this.

In those times, we often make things worse by trying to numb our pain through a pill bottle, shot glass or shopping spree. Sometimes we make decisions we instantly regret. Sometimes we try to distract ourselves, jumping into a hobby we have neither the time nor money for. Other times we withdraw altogether as a cloud of depression grows while we try to wait out the storms of life. In those times, we would give anything for a place of refuge, a place to let our wounds heal. If that describes you, the people in this book understand exactly what you are going through and have shared their stories because they want to help *you* find what they have found.

The thing is, refuge is found not in a place, but in a person — Christ. "God is our refuge and strength, an ever-present help in trouble." This may sound too good to be true. God knows I was skeptical the first time I heard this. I didn't grow up in the church, and by nature, I am pretty cynical. I'd heard lots of stories about churches and church people, and as I grew older, I grew even more skeptical.

It would be really easy to turn this book into an infomercial for our church (yes, these are stories from some of the people in our church). It would be easy to promise that if you would only pray a little prayer and get up a little earlier on Sunday morning, or squeeze in a worship service on a Saturday night, that all of your problems would be solved, all your hurts healed and life will be perfect. Sometimes it happens that way, but most of the time, it's simply not that simple.

While we love our church, this book isn't about us. This book isn't about growing the Ridgefield Church of the Nazarene. Quite frankly, our parking lot is already full, our classrooms already crowded and we already have to hold four services every weekend to make room for all of those who have experienced the reality of a new hope and a new future (although there is always room for you). We wanted to do this book because we know how hard life can be and because you are our neighbors. We see you everywhere. Our kids go to school together and play sports together. We see each other around town, we smile and nod and keep moving. You don't see our scars, we don't see yours and on the surface it looks like we all live in Mayberry, but we know that it's simply not that simple, and life is not a 1960s sitcom.

God loves us, all of us, regardless of where we have been, what we have done or what has been done to us. We know he is our refuge and our strength, and we would love nothing more than to share with you the hope we have found.

We are not a church of perfect people, and I am not a perfect pastor. We are simply real people, trying to figure out how to live the lives we were meant to live. We want you to know that our doors are nearly always open. Really. Maybe you used to be part of a church and had a bad experience. If that is you, I am so sorry that happened. I think most churches try really hard to be the kind of people God called them to be, but every once in a while, we Christians really mess it up, and I hope you will give the church a second chance.

Maybe you used to be part of a church, but life got in the way, and it's been a while; we would love to have you come back and join in again in what God is doing. Maybe you just have some questions about God, life, the Bible, but have never had the opportunity to ask someone. We would love to talk with you. Honestly, these are some of our favorite conversations. We promise not to preach at you, but we will answer your questions honestly. Feel free to email, call or if you have already met me (Pastor Brian) or one of our other leaders, feel free to stop us around town and ask.

Maybe you aren't quite ready for a conversation, but you are curious — feel free to listen in on our services online at www.ridgenaz.org, see some of the ministries we offer or join us for one of the many community events in which we participate.

Though we are part of a worldwide denomination, we are a family-friendly community church with multiple generations of people in every service. You are even welcome to pop in during the week and pick up a free Bible, grab a cup of coffee, take a quick tour of our building and browse our food pantry and clothing closet just to get a better sense of who we are.

Maybe you are ready to take that next step and join us for a service to learn more about Christ and the refuge he offers. We would love to have you come to our bilingual service (Spanish/English) on Friday night or one of our worship services, on Saturday evening at 6:30 or Sunday at 9 or 11:10 a.m. I know it can be scary thinking about going to a church; even I get nervous going to a new church, and I am a pastor. We would love to have you join us! Don't worry about being "the new person." We have new people every week, and it's hard to tell who's new and who has been here for years.

Our prayer for you is that this book would give you hope that there is a refuge. His name is Christ, and he is the God of new beginnings and second chances. Whether you join us or one of God's other churches (we're all on

CONCLUSION

the same team), we hope you will find a place of refuge in him so that your wounds can heal and your scars can become a reminder not of the fact that you were wounded, but of the fact that you have been healed.

Thanks for reading this book. We really do look forward to getting to know you better in the days ahead.

Pastor Brian R. Thomas
Ridgefield Church of the Nazarene

We would love for you to join us at Ridgefield Church of the Nazarene!

We meet Saturday evenings at 6:30 p.m. and Sunday mornings at 9 and 10:30 a.m. at 747 Pioneer Street, Ridgefield, WA 98642.

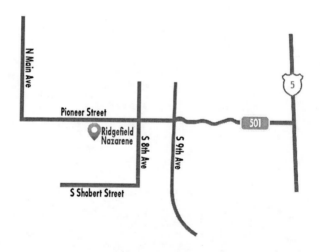

Contact Information
Phone: 360.887.3576
Website: www.ridgenaz.org
Email: office@ridgefieldnazarene.org

For more information on reaching your city with
stories from your church, go to
www.testimonybooks.com.

GOOD CATCH
PUBLISHING